Roger Law was born and brough
When Law left school aged 14 his headmaster hoped he would learn one thing in life; some manners.

Law made his escape from the family construction firm by going to art school in Cambridge, where he met Peter Fluck, who would collaborate with him on many projects, including the satirical puppet show *Spitting Image*, of which Mrs Thatcher claimed 'I don't ever watch that programme.' This, however, was no impediment to the nation eagerly tuning in to watch the Establishment being ridiculed, lampooned and bitingly satirised week after week.

Law just about survived the show's entire roller-coaster ride, eventually finding the brakes in 1997, after which he closed the factory gates, sold the puppets and bought a surfboard and a one-way ticket to Australia to start a new life. In Sydney he secured something like a base as 'artist in residence' in the Bondi Pavillion – a surfboard away from the famous beach.

Rarely in residence, Law spends most of his time travelling around and drawing that sunburnt country. Some of the fruits of these travels were featured in his exhibitions at the Rebecca Hossack Gallery and The Fine Art Society in London.

So is there life beyond redundancy? He'll let you know when he finds the time.

Collaborative writer on this book was Lewis Chester.

'Between [Roger Law and Lewis Chester], they have garnished Law's jolly life story with diverting details ... Law sounds like he's having far too much fun in the sun to risk a return to gloomy British satire. But his superb illustrations suggest that, should he ever tire of Bondi Beach, another brilliant career awaits back home in the periodicals that spawned his grotesque yet loveable effigies.'

Independent, William Cook

'Many glorious illustrations ... litter this book ... [it] is worth buying just for the twin studies of kangaroos. Not that it isn't a marvellous read. *Still Spitting at Sixty* is that rare thing, a ghost-written book that somehow distils its "writer's" essential flavour ... Hazlitt said we applaud satirists not out of love but fear. Impossible, though, to read this book and not love its author. Partly this is because it is so pungently amusing, partly because it is so unsickeningly life-affirming.'

Sunday Times, Christopher Bray

'This is really a sublime autobiography ... [it contains] some of the finest pieces of writing about Australia. Much more evocative than Bill Bryson. And the illustrations are wonderful.'

Sydney Morning Herald

'Highly engaging ... a breeze, a pleasure to read, as it leaps from anecdote to anecdote with aplomb and much humour. Like all the best people, Law is a dedicated fan of P.G. Wodehouse, and there are some lovely jokes here, if not the awesomely polished prose of his hero. This is a much more distinctive piece of work than the usual run of showbiz memoirs. And yet there is clearly something going on underneath ... great entertainment, and his paintings, which somehow manage to be both bold and delicate, are quite something.'

Daily Mail, Marcus Berkmann

'Filled with all the lunacy and flair that one would expect from the co-producer and creator of *Spitting Image*.'

Guardian

'This entertaining memoir takes the reader behind the scenes at *Spitting Image* and on to a series of hilarious adventures as a "teenage granddad" in the Outback of Australia.'

Sunday Express

ROGER LAW
WITH LEWIS CHESTER

STILL SPITTING AT SIXTY

FROM THE '60s TO MY SIXTIES, A SORT OF AUTOBIOGRAPHY

HarperCollins*Publishers*

HarperCollins*Entertainment*
An Imprint of HarperCollins*Publishers*
77–85 Fulham Palace Road,
Hammersmith, London W6 8JB

www.harpercollins.co.uk

This paperback edition 2006

First published in Great Britain by
HarperCollins*Entertainment* 2005

ISBN 978-0-00-718250-3

Set in Sabon

Find out more about HarperCollins and the environment at
www.harpercollins.co.uk/green

This book is dedicated to Richard Bennett, who is as essential to this sorry tale as Jiminy Cricket is to Pinocchio. Why didn't I listen?

'I can only see it going one way, that's my way. How it's actually going I have no idea.'

With apologies to Nick Wilshire (boxer)

CONTENTS

CHAPTER ONE

THE LiZARD OF OZ

I put my money on a blue-tongued lizard called Eternal Youth, and lost a packet. To be fair, it had legged it bravely in the early stages of the race, but seemed to lose its way around the half-way stage before completely running out of puff. It eventually came in a distant, and dismal, fifth.

My instinctive first thought was that my lizard had been drugged or 'nobbled'. Such practices were not unheard of in Eulo near Cunnamulla, Queensland, where the Lizard Race ranks as one of the highest events in the annual sporting calendar. But, on reflection, I think that Eternal Youth simply buckled under the weight of my expectations.

It was perhaps not eternal youth I was after (well, too late for

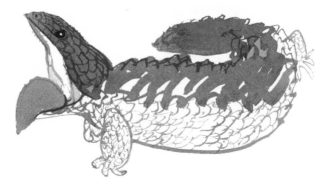

that), but it was true that I had come to Australia in a quest for a new lease of life.

A few months earlier I had joined the ranks of the functionally obsolete – a fast-expanding tribe, composed of people whose main purpose in life has expired through such mechanisms as redundancy, forced early retirement or just sheer bad luck. Yet these are people who still, if the actuarial tables are to be believed, have a lot of existence in prospect. And no clear idea of what to do with it.

I found myself very thoroughly washed up when the satire bubble burst and I was obliged to dismantle the engine of public mockery called *Spitting Image* which I had spent most of the previous twenty years carefully assembling. For all its faults, some of which I am now ready to admit, and even elaborate upon, *Spitting Image* was an engrossing way of life. The business of squeezing anarchic, disrespectful humour into a series of high-pressure deadlines meant that I was rarely afflicted with the problem of leisure. If I ever had a day off I can't remember it because I was either asleep or seeking refuge in tired and emotional behaviour.

The end was not exactly of my choosing, though I always

knew there had to be one. Fashions in satire, like anything else, come and go, and ours could be no exception. But when our satirical fad was over it exposed an unusually large number of rudderless satirists with a tendency to live on. Fortunately, most of those who worked for me churning out the puppets and other grotesques in the *Spitting Image* workshop were lucky enough to be exploited child labourers, fresh out of art school in many cases. When our show was done they were able to go on and find new, and usually more profitable, avenues for their talents in showbiz or the arts. Youth was on their side. But the way ahead for the boss, poor soul, was not so evident. Nobody's heart bled for him, of course. After all I'd had what is called 'a bloody good run'. But there I was, jobless at 56, too young to retire and too old to be retrained, and without any discernible talent for domesticity or addressing a golf ball.

As the business wound down, I had naturally explored other options. I did not feel quite ready for the job of marshalling the supermarket trolleys outside my local Safeway (though I have it in mind for later on), so I looked around in what might be called my field of art education. A couple of art college interviews convinced me, and my interviewers, that I could never achieve the level of bureaucratic expertise required these days to bring on the young. I was nonetheless attracted by the Royal College of Art's suggestion that I might set up a new animation course for advanced students. But developments in animation are now incredibly fast and this, combined with problems of establishing a new set-up, would, I realized, make for a job as taxing as *Spitting Image* had been. I was just not ready for another ordeal.

I felt fit enough, but mentally I was knackered. It was slowly dawning on me that what I wanted was not so much a specific job but a rekindled enthusiasm. The stuff I had before *Spitting Image* inexorably turned me into a harassed, 'kick-ass' capitalist. The trouble was that I had become way too business-wise for my own good. There were, I felt, artistic sides of me virtually neglected since my art school days which I would really like to develop now that I had the time and opportunity. But the business side of me said, 'Forget it. There's no market.' And was I really prepared to go traipsing round the galleries and art establishments with my folder of fledgling menopausal artwork trying to drum up commissions from people whose fathers might have worked for me, or even been fired by me? The mere prospect seemed fraught with possibilities of satire at my expense. Perish the thought.

To begin again, it seemed I really needed a place or circumstance where I had no reputation and effectively no past to live down or up to. Hence my decision to transport myself to Australia.

As it happened, my day in Eulo was anything but blighted by the poor performance of Eternal Youth. Among those who commiserated with me about my lizard's lack of staying power was a tall, elderly man wearing a hat festooned with crocodile teeth, who turned out to be the town's most famous citizen, the Aboriginal writer Herb Wharton.

Author of a string of yarns with titles like *Where Ya' Been, Mate?*, Wharton had a Solomon-like reputation. A cattle drover in his youth, he is now a kind of cultural drover, having walked about all over Australia, and a couple of neighbouring continents besides. Sponsored by R.M. Williams, the quintessentially Aussie outfitters, and dressed in their outback best – leather boots, moleskins, check shirt and Akubra hat –

Herb Warton

Wharton exudes an ambassadorial charm such that he has been known to set off on world lecture tours with just a $20 bill in his back pocket and to return three months later with the same dollar bill still intact.

Herb, who became a friend, was happy to apply his considerable mind to my situation. If I wanted to experience a new life, he said, I should make a point of getting out of the cities – there were different, mind-expanding worlds to be savoured in the outback. And, now that I had got my eye in by starting to paint again, I should be better placed than most to appreciate this fact. If I wanted to take him up on the offer, he said, he could introduce me to extraordinary parts of Australia, virtually unknown to the white man, that would blow my mind (though he couldn't absolutely guarantee that David Attenborough had not at one time passed through with a film crew).

Herb later proved as good as his word. But at the time he struck a note of caution, warning me not to expect too much of anything, on account of things being a bit crook for all of us from the very beginning. And the fault, he thought, was entirely God's. If only he had had the sense to create Adam and Eve as Aborigines, there would have been no such thing as the Fall of Man. An Aboriginal Eve, for sure, would have eaten the snake in preference to the pippin.

CHAPTER TWO

FEN BOY

My original sin was to be born in Littleport, a tiny town-cum-village struggling to keep its head above water in the heart of the Fens on the border between Norfolk and Cambridgeshire. In these days of high-speed motorways and second homes it is hard to imagine just how cut off from the rest of the world the Fens seemed in those days. Or indeed, to imagine how strange the outside world seemed to its inhabitants. My father, who ran his own construction business, would tell me about the time he had taken his workforce up to London to see the sights. This was reckoned to be a great success by the men, who spent the whole day going up and down the escalators at Liverpool Street Station. As a child, the only part of this story that I found improbable was my father ever allowing his workers off site for an entire day.

I was a wartime baby, born on 6 September 1941, but I cannot claim to have shared much in the war's privations. Living close to the land we never went short, drawing nourishment from the acre of land we shared with an abundance of chickens, ducks, rabbits and a pig. At Sunday lunch it was my father's proud boast that the only purchased ingredient was the flour to make the Yorkshire pudding. My father was often away in the army but he was not exactly a fund of conventional war stories on his returns to the comforts of home. By all accounts he spent more of his time fighting his own officers than he did fighting Hitler. A high proportion of his military service was spent in the glasshouse.

I have two graphic memories from my infancy. One was of a huge scary effigy of Hitler being burned in the centre of Littleport. That really was impressive, but not quite so entrancing as the visual experience I had when my father had the job of painting the Burnham Overy Staithe windmill. Before applying the pitch to the brickwork, he had me securely strapped to the windmill's upper balcony. From this vantage I could look far out to sea through the tumbling sails. Magical.

Even as a child in the Fens you had a sense of living on the edge. There was always the feeling that the water might reclaim the land and that Littleport's 4,000 inhabitants could be engulfed or, if they were lucky, resume their status as an island people. As kids we would go out with poles to certain fields and poke the apparently solid surface of the earth. Three or four feet down it would be like jelly. And if the place did not sink without trace, there seemed a good chance it would be blown away by the icy winds that came howling across the open spaces, straight from Siberia. At almost any time of the year the Fens could whip up a penetrating damp that chilled to the marrow. I don't think I've ever been really cold since I left.

The character of the people was less wintry than the terrain, but it was to some extent shaped by it. From Roman times the Fen country has been a natural refuge for outlaws, as the bogs deterred hot pursuit by the forces of law and order. Hereward the Wake held out against the Norman invaders in the marshes around Ely before he was betrayed by a greedy abbot. In Regency times the Fens were a popular hideout for runaway black slaves, which accounts for some of today's more exotic physiognomies.

The inaccessibility of the area was also prized by its more law-abiding inhabitants, who could comfortably subsist there by trapping, shooting and fishing the teeming water-lands. When they started to drain the Fens, there was no end of problems with the local labour hired to do the work. They would dig the trenches for money by day, and fill them in at night for free to deter the onset of progress. They were the original Fen Tigers. Eventually Irish navvies had to be brought in.

The works of central government were regarded with distrust, sometimes with good reason. It was a rising in Littleport that sparked the bread riots round the country in the wake of the Napoleonic Wars. These were stamped out with great ferocity. The officer in charge of quelling the disturbances was quoted as saying, 'Last year the battle of Waterloo, this year the battle of Hullabaloo.' In 1816 five Littleport men were hanged for their part in the rioting. I was acquainted with many of their descendants.

A sense of being at odds with the world beyond the Fens, even though many people made a living by selling produce to it, was very much a part of my upbringing. One consequence of this peculiar solidarity was that there was not a lot of class feeling, though some were richer than others. Nor was there much in the way of professional arrogance. The ranks of Fenland doctors and dentists seemed to contain an unusually large number of people who had been chucked out of the Royal Navy. Nor, it must be acknowledged, was there much in the way of cultural diversity.

Growing up in Littleport, my first artistic inspiration was Mr Baumber, the sign-writer. The most impressive thing about Mr Baumber was not so much the excellence of his signs but the casual elegance of his way of life. Unlike my father and my uncles, he seemed to exist very much on his own terms. The little work that he did he seemed to enjoy, and the rest of the time he would be pleasantly inebriated. You could say, in modern psychological parlance, that he was my first serious role model.

Even Mr Baumber's imperfections had charm. It was said that his one serious deficiency as a sign-writer was a tendency to spell in a highly individual way. Thus when he painted the sign for my father's building business, Law Brothers Building Constructors, his version came out as 'Law Brothers Building Constrictors'. I later came to feel that Mr Baumber may have grasped an essential truth about the enterprise.

Remnants of past ways of life and death were still in evidence when I was a child. Old people still drank poppy tea to ease the ague and the irritation of mosquitoes. There was also talk of the special brew, the black teapot, which I gathered – I don't think incorrectly – was designed to help those who had become a burden to their families on their way into the next world. I would have nightmares about this vessel which I managed to exorcise later in life by making one. This black teapot – festooned with poisonous scorpions, spiders and snakes – is now on view in Norwich Castle Museum.

My family's tradition was essentially muscular. My grandfather, Robert, had an iconic status long after his death, which occurred when my own father was eight years old. He had originally been a blacksmith with a sideline in breaking horses, before making a great success as a general dealer. He invested all his money in cattle and a large chunk of Welney Wash. He prospered to the extent of opening a couple of butcher's shops in the village and even sold his meat pies in London. His business was then completely wiped out by drought, quickly followed by a foot and mouth epidemic. Soon after, he died a typical Fenland death. A horse and carriage crashed through the ice on the Wash and my grandfather helped rescue the trapped driver. He then went home and died of pneumonia.

He had thirteen children, eleven surviving, and these were

farmed out among different families in Littleport, which gave me a tremendous range of aunts and uncles as a child. The Laws were a rather stoic breed, without being dour, and also quite ambitious, none more so than my father.

My father, I often felt, was a driven man, and the drive was to restore the fortune that fate had so cruelly wrested from the grasp of his own father. At various times he had three other brothers, Bill, Jack and Felix, working with him in the construction business, which hugely profited from the post-war council housing boom. But there were absolutely no family favours. The workers were expected to work at the double, but George Law's nearest and dearest were expected to die for the business.

The more cosmopolitan side of my upbringing came from my mother, Winifred, and her family, the Hiblins. My mother's parents ran the dairy in Littleport but they were acquainted with a much wider world. They had run a shop in the East End of London and my grandmother Jenny had worked in Birmingham for many years, in a supervisory capacity in the rag trade. She knew all the old music hall songs and was a lot of fun, if a bit sharp with it. Her husband was more subdued, but not unimpressive. Wilfrid had served in the First World War, and had lived to tell the tale, though with some difficulty. While he was on ambulance duty on the front line, part of his jaw had been shot away.

On weekends I would help out on the milk rounds. This involved venturing down tracks with names like Burnt Fen and Coffee Drove to lonely black pitched shacks and Fletton brick bungalows, flagged by a couple of desolate poplars as windbreaks. To survive this specialized work it was necessary to judge, within a gnat's whisker, the length of the ubiquitous Alsatian's chain.

My reward was getting to sit with my grandmother on
Saturday evenings when, gin bottle to hand, she would do the
books at a table covered with piles of coins and wads of notes.

With the accounting done I was allowed to work my way through several bottles of Ely Ales from the crate in the pantry. Pleasantly inebriated, I would then listen to grandma's tales of big city life, and get to sing some of the old songs along with her, the bawdier the better. My all-time favourites were 'A Little Bit of What You Fancy Does You Good' and the more intricate 'Keep Your Hand on Your Ha'penny, and Hold Your Ha'penny Tight'.

My grandparents were also remarkable for being among the first people in the neighbourhood to own a television set, and I can remember, aged 12, being forced to watch a snowstorm on it called 'The Coronation' when I wanted to be out in the fields with my dog, Scrap, looking for birds' nests. This undoubtedly damaged any royalist tendencies I might have had.

There was an unspoken but implicit assumption among the Hiblins that my mother, who had been to grammar school in Ely, had married slightly beneath her station. Apparently my father had wooed and won her by clambering over seven rows of seats in the Empire cinema, Littleport, to be by her side. He was seen as a man of purpose, but perhaps a shade uncouth. Politically, the Hiblins were quite sophisticated and refined, being of the Liberal persuasion.

My father's political outlook is something I still find hard to define. From the frequency with which he said a problem could be solved by shooting somebody, you might think he was a Fascist. At the same time he had nothing but contempt for what could be described as the professional shooting classes, like the army for example. Military service, to his way of thinking, never made a man of anybody. Soldiers were not encouraged to think for themselves and became essentially lazy. His firmest belief was in work, and it would be hard to find a more instinctive capitalist, or a man more totally wedded to the proposition that people should pull themselves up by their own bootstraps. And his offspring were expected to demonstrate similar convictions. He had some time for Oliver Cromwell, Fenland's greatest gift to Puritanism, but his real hero was the contractor Sir Robert McAlpine, whose dying words, according to my father, were, 'Keep the big mixer rolling, boys.'

Yet when the Tories were in power they would be denigrated as 'Them' as opposed to 'Us'. Like many people in the Fens, he was fiercely anti-authority while being quite a considerable authority figure himself. While I was growing up he always voted Labour, but he would have a late-flowering love affair with the politics of Mrs Thatcher.

I probably learned more trying to figure out where my father was coming from than I ever did from school, where I was mainly distinguished for my misbehaviour. After the Three Rs, education in the Fens did not seem to lead anywhere much. In those days there were eight grammar school places reserved for 11-plus successes in the whole Isle of Ely. There did not seem much point in trying, particularly when Littleport Secondary Modern had a reputation for being a good laugh.

When I first went there the headmaster's favourite activity was playing the violin to the accompaniment of Fenland bird-song whistled by the boys. Unfortunately he left, to be replaced by Mr Browning, who had the much more ridiculous notion of turning the enterprise into a mini public school with houses, prefects and all that nonsense. I could not take to it, so I became disruptive. I would invite trouble by saying 'Hello' instead of 'Yes, Sir' when the register was being called, and I was caned for each offence until the form master got bored with hitting me. As I had no time for homework I rarely had any answers in the classroom, though the sullenness of my responses did help to sharpen up Mr Browning's satirical skills. 'Say something, Law,' he would counsel, by way of encouragement, 'if it's only "Goodbye".'

One new master marked our first encounter by belting me across the room and saying, 'Now, Law, you can do one thing wrong.' My reputation for making teachers' lives a misery had evidently preceded me, and he was getting his retaliation in first.

My real education was in the holidays when, as the elder son, I was expected to immerse myself in the ways of the family business. That meant working with my father and his brothers on the building sites, where health and safety regulations were honoured only in the breach. On a Law Brothers', more popularly known as Claw Brothers', site everything was done on piece rates at breakneck speed, and if there was a corner to be cut my father would cut it. It was said of him that he did not lay bricks so much as 'throw them down'. We would recycle track from disused railway lines, doors from old Nissen huts – anything that could be scavenged. We used wooden scaffolding, long past its day, and any deep trenches on site would routinely be left dangerously unsupported. The firm had acquired a reputation as the fastest contract builders in the East and my father aimed to keep it, whatever the building regulations might say. All this frantic activity would be laced with George Law's special line in inspirational messages for the workers, all variants on, 'If the dog hadn't stopped for a crap he'd have caught the hare.'

If the building inspector came by asking who was the governor, we were trained to say, 'We're all the boss here.' I remember that one inspector, more tenacious than most, managed to

figure out that the man aloft bricking the chimney was the boss. So he took off after my father, shinning up one of our typical ramshackle structures, and caused the whole thing to collapse. He fell and broke both ankles, while my father stayed aloft, secure with his chimney.

Any impediments to the flow of work somehow melted away. I remember there was what seemed like a problem with a 70-acre parcel of land near Mildenhall, prime construction territory but for the preservation order on the Saxon barn and moat it contained. A mysterious fire removed the chief obstacle, and my father's men promptly set to work building what is, as far as I am aware, the only moated council estate in England. Local gypsies were blamed for setting the fire, but I sensed that they may not have been the prime movers.

One day Uncle Bill had a heart attack on a roof. We had two pulleys, one of which worked fine but the other was known to be dodgy. As we were preparing to lower him with the sound mechanism, Uncle Jack's voice floated up from below: 'Don't put him there, boys. We're bringing up the bricks.' So the sick man went down on the dodgy pulley, fortunately without mishap.

On another day my young brother Martin broke several ribs when the Law Brothers work bus, en route to a distant site, slewed off the road into a river bank. Minutes after the crash, with Martin and the workers slumped dazed and bloodied by the crumpled bus, Uncle Jack came by in his car. Martin can remember his first words of succour to this day: 'If anyone wants to work, they can get in the car and come with me.'

Episodes of this kind began to concentrate my young mind. Long before I left school I had been acquainted with most of the trials and terrors of a construction worker's life. I had worked incredibly long hours, staggering around under a hod full of bricks, longing to hear Uncle Jack's familiar call for one last push: 'The day is short, and the night is long, so get along my old beauties.' I had enjoyed the experience of having my hands stuck fast by the hoar frost to scaffolding clamps, and having to prise them off with warm tea. I had crumpled under the weight of a concrete lintel and all but gone off the edge of the scaffolding. My Uncle Jack grabbed me and saved me, without saying a word. I got the impression that this was business as usual, so I went down and got another lintel.

The annual light relief was Feast Day, the main public holiday for the farming community Littleport when people came from all around to show off their heavy horses and their most exquisite vegetables. There would be little competition tents in which people could demonstrate their prowess. I would show a few rabbits and some drawings which invariably won first or second prize. There was also a beer tent which stayed open all day, and by the close of play it would be a seething mass of flesh and tattoos. In later life I introduced my Aboriginal Australian friend, Herb Wharton, to a Littleport Feast Day celebration. He was kind enough to say, 'It's just like the outback, mate.'

Very occasionally I would mention to my father that the work at Law Brothers did seem rather hard, but this would only lead to an early version of the *Monty Python* sketch in which the participants brag competitively about the awfulness of their origins. Whatever I might have suffered, he had suffered ten times worse. I couldn't even begin to know what tiredness was. Why, in his young days he had been so knackered that when he got one leg out of bed in the morning he had to put it back in to get the other one out. To me this sounded like quite a gymnastic achievement for an exhausted young man, but it was usually best to let my father win such arguments.

At the same time, he was not an unkind man. He did not, for example, think I should go into the world defenceless. Sometimes, without my mother's knowledge, we would sneak off to Chatteris where there was a boxing club, made famous by Eric Boon who became the British welterweight champion. I was shown the ropes there and introduced to the Noble Art.

Family holidays would be spent on the North Norfolk coast among the sand dunes and the broad sweep of reed marshes at places that I still think of as the acceptable face of the Fens. The North Norfolk coast in summer seemed to us a world away from the bleak Fenland winters. Initially we made day trips to Holme, Old Hunstanton and Wells-next-the-Sea. Later, as my father made money, we would take a week's holiday in places

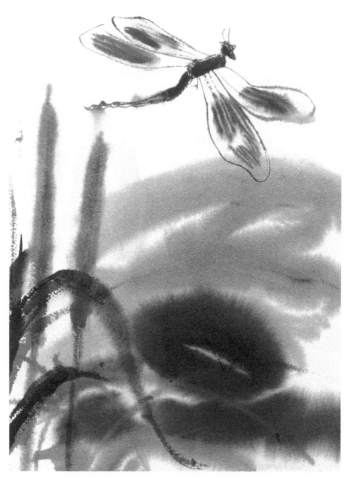

like Sheringham and Cromer. My brother and I would net shrimps and butterflies and go cockling on the mudflats where my father would haul out crabs, big as dinner plates, from under the rocks until the tide turned. Then it would be home to boil up the shrimps until they were as red and ready to peel as the skin on our backs and faces. In Cromer I even managed to get a smattering of religious education from the evangelists who held prayer meetings on the beach, competing with the *Punch and Judy* show for the holiday-makers' attention. I can distinctly remember Martin and myself enthusiastically singing 'Jesus Wants Me for a Sunbeam', possibly because it seemed like an agreeable alternative occupation to the world of work as we knew it.

Even on holiday my father was an active man, dedicated to improving some aspect of himself or his sons. He was a strong swimmer and a keen diver, specializing in the swallow dive (you throw both arms back like wings and arch your back in imitation of a bird). He was teaching me how to do this from a breakwater at high tide when, intent on maintaining my wing spread, I hit my head on the breakwater's hidden prop. I then drifted unconscious out to sea until I was hauled back by father who, when I came round, naturally insisted on my repeating the dive in case I lost my nerve.

Despite this and many other kindnesses, a powerful conviction was forming in my mind that fulfilling my father's expectations of me was just about the last thing I wanted to do on leaving school. The future leadership of the Law Brothers' construction empire would, I felt, be much better entrusted to young Martin. But my way out was not immediately apparent.

I had always liked to draw, but there did not seem to be much scope for earning an artistic living in Littleport, other than in the sign-writing area which Mr Baumber had cornered. I had always drawn for fun rather than as a career prospect, though the activity had brought me some local notoriety. One of my more ambitious designs was a large crayon portrait of

Clem Attlee, done on a hoarding, which had helped Labour to lose the 1951 General Election.

It was my mother who first grasped that this hobby of mine could provide my escape route. Though supportive of my father, she could at least entertain the notion that there could be more to her children's lives than the high-speed laying of brick on brick. She made some inquiries and discovered that it was possible then (though alas not now) to gain admittance to an art school on the strength of work done, without any formal qualifications. Accordingly I submitted a slim portfolio of my Feast Day studies to the Cambridge School of Art and was, to my great surprise, accepted.

I was not unhappy to take my leave of Littleport Secondary Modern, and the pleasure, it seemed, was wholly mutual. Mr Browning's last headmasterly words to me were: 'I don't know what will happen to you in life, but wherever you go I hope you will learn some manners.'

CHAPTER THREE

UNIVERSITY CHALLENGED

When I arrived at art school, still some days short of my fifteenth birthday, I thought I had died and gone to heaven. I had half feared that it would be like an extension of secondary school, but there was no catch as far as I could see. Within weeks I was smoking as many Woodbines as I could lay my hands on and getting to gaze, through my studies in Life Class, at a variety of naked women. Since I had not yet managed the art of joined-up handwriting, I knew my chances of emulating Mr Baumber's sign-writing skills were slim, but I did not mind that in the least, as I could instantly see many other far more exotic possibilities opening up before me.

In those less pressured days, before the Commercial Art course was renamed Graphic Design or Visual Culture, the

whole emphasis was on skills across a wide spectrum – drawing, sculpture, modelling, painting, ceramics, printmaking, stage design, lettering, you name it. No running before walking was allowed. Practising the skills, rather than writing or theorizing about them, was the order of the day. There was of course no question of acquaintance with what is now often considered the best friend of trainee designers and even artists – the computer.

It was a different world, ludicrously old-fashioned by today's standards, but it was one that left its mark. I may not have been the most disciplined of students, but to this day I can make a fair stab at identifying an artist's influences by looking at their work, pull an etching plate from the acid at the right moment, and when modelling think three-dimensionally without effort.

The course took four years, almost five in my case as I had some catching up to do. To compensate for the largely self-inflicted inadequacies of my Littleport education, I was initially put on a course of general literary and historical studies run by a man called David Joseph, who subsequently rose to great heights in the Open University. I did not come to this discipline with a wholly virgin brain as my mind was brimful of *Krazy Kat, L'il Abner* and numerous other American comics available in Littleport as surplus to the requirements of the surrounding US air bases like Mildenhall and Alconbury. Joseph enriched the mixture with injections of Dylan Thomas, John Steinbeck, J.D. Salinger and John Osborne, and in the process he gave me an appetite for literature that I could never have acquired in the regimented atmosphere of my old school. The fact that there were no mandatory examinations may also have helped, though I did take an O Level paper in History and passed, thanks to a heaven-sent question on the Littleport riots.

The art school, originally founded by John Ruskin, was quite small, with only about 100 pupils taught in groups of ten or twelve. The technical college, of which it formed a part in my day, was grafted on later and run on more sausage-machine lines. There were a quite a few Fenland potato-heads like myself on the technical side, but the art school exhibited a much wider social range. There were earnest grammar school types along with a generous sprinkling of public schoolboys whose company in the college, and in the university, I tended to prefer for their more irresponsible quality. We were also uplifted by the presence of some very upper-class girls with double-barrelled names, who had been sent to the Cambridge School of Art to find a husband, preferably from the university.

To the task of teaching this motley group the staff brought an admirable attention to detail. Some of the older tutors had been taught anatomy at the Slade by Henry Tonks, a man of legendary application. During the First World War Tonks had been asked about his feelings when he composed drawings of soldiers on the front line. 'It's a chamber of horrors,' Tonks said, 'but I am quite content to draw them as it is excellent practice.' In keeping with the Tonks tradition, we had to do drawings of absolutely gigantic magnifications of human ears, feet and hands which were much weirder than anything you might see on *Spitting Image*. The commitment of all our tutors was impressive, though few could excel John Norris-Wood, who took us for natural history drawing and kept a crocodile in his bath.

During my first year I grew very fast to well over 6 feet. As a result I would be looking around for fellows of my own age who might make useful drinking companions without giving me a crick in the neck. One morning in Life Class, at the start of the second year, I spotted what looked like a suitable case. He was a tall, fair-haired new boy who was looking at the model with that peculiar tense expression which indicated that he was gazing upon his first naked lady. I went up behind him and said, 'Hello mate, I come from Littleport.'

Peter Fluck was hardly my ideal as a friend. For one thing he was neither a fellow potato-head nor a public schoolboy. He was the son of a grocer and belonged to that despised breed, a grammar schoolboy, with four O Levels to prove it. We were almost exactly the same age but he had wasted the previous year at school amassing these impressive qualifications. The other galling thing about Fluck was that he was an absolute ace at lettering, with virtually no formal training. I used to ascribe this skill to the frequency with which he had to repaint the 'L' in the sign over his father's shop in Park Street.

I do not think I was Peter Fluck's ideal as a friend either. I think I was, and probably remained, a mite too boisterous and uncouth for his more refined taste. The thing that doomed us to each other's company was the fact that we made each other laugh.

Very shortly after our first meeting we left the bosoms of our respective families and set up as independent men of the world in a shambolic room in a house in Oxford Road. We would sleep there on opposite sides of a large double bed in chaste amity. Soon after this ménage had been established I took up with Deirdre Amsden, who was among the more capable students in our class and the possessor of a most entrancing bum. The consequence was that Deirdre moved in and Fluck found himself forced out of the room onto a mattress in the hallway. Fortunately, he had to laugh.

Life at college was enjoyably disrupted by the arrival of Alec Heath who, as the new principal, rapidly started to introduce new teachers. The man he brought in to ginger up drawing was Paul Hogarth, a descendant of the famous William, or so he said, though this was his least significant credential.

Unlike the men in the Tonks tradition, Hogarth was a really

Paul Hogarth

exciting character. He was not a career teacher but someone who had lived by selling his skills in the marketplace and this, Fluck and I decided, was very much the way we wanted to go. Hogarth also demonstrated the possibilities for combining art with action. He had travelled the world, drawing and politicking when the occasion demanded. He had driven relief lorries in the Spanish Civil War, and later in Poland in the 1940s. In the early 1950s he had been among the first to open up Eastern Europe and China to Western eyes through his drawings. Though identified with Communist causes, his work was most celebrated in the United States, where it appeared regularly in magazines like *Fortune* and *Sports Illustrated*.

He was also appealing to us for the way he had mislaid his first wife. She had told him that if he worked with 'yet another drunken writer' she would be on her way. As it happened, Hogarth had accepted a commission to do the illustrations for a book about Ireland, working in collaboration with Brendan Behan, one of the island's thirstiest inhabitants. The book was a great success, but it was the end of the marriage.

It was through Hogarth that we became acquainted with the concept of the 'artist reporter', essentially an artist dealing with the topical issues of the day as raw material. This was immensely appealing as I was drawn to the idea of making visual statements rather than just representations. And I was already dabbling in caricature. This was not one of Hogarth's areas of expertise but, unlike his predecessors, he encouraged this form of expression. Indeed, he went so far as to publicize one of his own exhibitions with a caricature of himself done by me. This was a brave act considering that his hairstyle was not dissimilar to Bobby Charlton's.

Hogarth taught us that there are a million ways of portraying the world, and that these endless possibilities had to be tailored to the artist's vision. Young artists used to be apprenticed to older artists not so much for technical reasons but in order to achieve the approved focus. Taking this message to heart, I became very adept at achieving Hogarth's focus, making the marks he made and, more importantly, omitting what he would leave out. One day, in a bid to test the limits of his sense of humour, I copied a drawing he was working on while he was out to lunch. I then scrunched it up and threw it on the floor, while concealing the original inside his desk. Naturally he found the scrunched version first. He went ape, until I revealed the switch. But he was not a man to hold a grudge. Soon afterwards, as if in recognition of my plagiaristic skill, he began to steer paying work in my direction – small commissions from the *East Anglian* magazine and other local publications which he could not get around to doing. These little sub-Hogarthian studies constituted my first published work.

Another teacher who impressed us deeply was Bobby Hunt, who had worked closely with Fitzrovia's star illustrator and painter, John Minton. Indeed, it was said that Minton would offload surplus work to Hunt and later sign it as being his own. Hunt's classes were like stand-up comedy routines, though he knew his stuff. He was also a boozer but avoided alcohol addiction, it was suggested, by never closing his mouth long enough to swallow his drinks. As he taught he used to pace the studio's parquet floor. This endless pacing worked some of the blocks loose and one day he tripped, and both he and one of the blocks flew across the room. On replacing the woodblock, he found a tightly folded note had been placed underneath it. As he stood up he carefully unfolded the note and read aloud to the class, 'Bobby Hunt is a cunt.' I could not claim any credit for this particular wheeze but I had to admire the foresight, skill and planning that must have gone into its execution.

Paul Hogarth's greatest gift to us was access to his library. Both Fluck and I were already well versed in the English tradition – Gillray, Cruikshank and the rest – but Hogarth had an enormous range of European stuff that we had never clapped eyes on. We would descend on his home at weekends and devour back issues of *L'Assiette au Beurre* (which colloquially translates as *Gravy Train*), the brainchild of Samuel Schwarz, a Polish Jew who made his original stake by selling soft porn in

French garrison towns. The best illustrations were to be found in the early twentieth-century numbers, where all the issues of the day – from concentration camps to the Dreyfus Affair – were confronted with fierce satirical energy. And Hogarth would show us books of drawings by George Grosz about Hitler's Germany in the 1930s which were so powerful they gave you the feeling of almost being there.

The most practical thing Hogarth helped to provide was contacts. He got on to the university and told them there was no reason why their publications should all look so execrable when there were so many able art students resident in the same town. Partly as a result, Deirdre and I got to art-edit a number of university organs, including six issues of *Granta*, a young thinking person's magazine if ever there was one. Our successor on *Granta* was Peter Fluck.

There was a pretty girl in our year called Wendy Snowdon who fell in love with, and later married, an undergraduate by the name of Peter Cook. So we all became friendly. All over Cambridge at that time I would hear young men talking with oddly depressed vowels (later nationally recognized as the key intonation of Cook's E.L. Wisty creation) and I was relieved to meet the originator of this strange voice. I was beginning to fear it might be contagious. Cook was a funny man, but you would hardly have picked him as the father figure of the satire revolution that was lurking just around the corner. He already had the laconic delivery that he would bring to some of his later more famous observations – 'my lady wife, whose name escapes me', 'not a million miles from the truth' and 'tragically, I was born an only twin' – but he did not give the impression of being a man of great initiative. In appearance then he was like a Regency buck, but pleasantly diffident with it. If he had a keen interest,

Peter Cook

other than the horse-racing pages of the national newspapers, I never noticed what it was. But he became a kind of benefactor.

Cook owned a building in Park Street, a few doors down from Fluck's grocery store, and it had some surplus space. He allowed Fluck, Deirdre and myself to occupy the ground floor and to put up a Fluck-fashioned sign announcing that East Anglian Artists was open for business. Since neither Fluck nor I was on a grant, we both came under a certain amount of parental pressure to earn a few bob. My father tended to treat me with all the reverence that he might accord to an out-of-work actor, though he could never quite bring himself to wish me out of college and into the army, an ever-present possibility since conscription was still in force. East Anglian Artists, being on a flight path to Cook, who lived upstairs, attracted some intriguing visitors. One was David Frost, though there was never a lot of point in knowing Frost if you already knew Cook because he would retell all Cook's jokes. Cook called him 'the bubonic plagiarist'.

East Anglian Artists never did much actual business. Nor, for that matter, did our movie. This was a delicate study of Deirdre and myself as two beautiful young people with Fluck brilliantly empathizing the role of an imbecilic old man. Shot on location in a country house and a scrap metal yard, it was taken to New York by its student director in search of a niche market. Neither he nor the film has been heard of since.

Eventually Fluck and I discovered that we could make more serious money by doing the early-morning cleaning at Fitzwilliam House and by waiting at table for the undergraduates at Trinity, where we became celebrated as the 'Gypsy Menace'. It was therefore not very long before self-service catering was introduced.

For all our reverses on the economic front, we were rarely idle. The late 1950s were the early days of the peace movement, which reached its crescendo with the Aldermaston marches. Many of us were deeply involved in the Campaign for Nuclear Disarmament (CND) and its later more aggressive offshoot, the Committee of 100, which had a deliberate policy of direct action, including breaking the law of the land. There were some staid figures in the college who saw this as evidence that Hogarth was leading the young astray, but it was not so. Hogarth had by this time left the Communist Party a disillusioned man. The one thing he never wanted to talk about was contemporary politics.

It is hard, looking back, to recapture the intensity and anger of that period. I think it boiled down to a feeling that we had been hoodwinked about the nature and extent of the nuclear threat. When you stripped away all the reassuring rhetoric about nuclear war being 'limited' you realized that this meant limited to Britain and a few others who had drawn short straws in Europe. No matter how limited any nuclear conflict was, you could be sure that Littleport, with its friendly neighbourhood US bomber bases, would have no chance. Later generations would learn how to become more fatalistic about the nuclear threat but mine was idealistic, or perhaps innocent, enough to believe that things could be changed.

Blessed with a grandfather who was deeply versed in the horrors of war and who seemed only too delighted to pay my fines, I became a none-too-pacific peace agitator. My time spent being picked on in pubs as a serious underage drinker had equipped me well for the confrontational stuff to which every demonstration is prone, while my art school training was all I needed by way of entrance to the crude but exciting world of agitprop.

David Joseph, my literary mentor at college, had a friend called Richard Fletcher who paved the way. Fletcher was a very intriguing man who had invented a method for sticking aluminium on to plastic and paper. You can see examples of its application in the average packet of peanuts. Unfortunately for Fletcher, he patented the machine that churned the stuff out rather than the process itself, and missed out on a gold mine in royalties. Aside from being a distraught inventor, he was also an ex-racing car driver for Lotus, a property developer, the publisher of newspaper called *Union Voice*, and a Labour Party fixer of a very high order. Fletcher was aiming to fix things so that the Labour Party would come out in favour of unilateral nuclear disarmament, which indeed it did at the Scarborough Conference in 1960 (only to do a U-turn a year later).

Fluck and I, together with several other mates at college, supplied the artistic shock effects for Fletcher's posters and pamphlets, indicting Hugh Gaitskell and the right-wing Labour leadership for all its revisionist works. Fletcher, in his turn, provided logistical support, in the form of a van. We would use this to travel to the big union and party conferences, where we would plaster the neighbourhood, with special reference to the delegates' bedroom and breakfast room windows, with our compelling messages.

These trips took some organizing. I can remember one raid on a Labour Party conference quite vividly as it was the time when we made the stew. There were twelve us going in Fletcher's van and as nobody seemed to have any money I had the bright idea of filling a milk churn with a gigantic stew of cabbage and pigs' trotters that would sustain us through a week's agitation. There was no problem locating a milk churn, but the process of cooking the stew and decanting it by stages into the churn proved incredibly lengthy – so lengthy, in fact, that by the time the last pigs' trotters had gone in at the top those at the bottom had gone off, infecting the whole brew. We then had the problem of burying eighty pints of pigs' trotter stew in a Cambridge garden. This was done under cover of night, and to the best of my knowledge the stew remains buried there to this day. At some future date, no doubt, it will make a most interesting archaeological find.

I never ceased to enjoy art college, but it was becoming evident that some aspects of my existence were getting up the nose of the authorities. There was much twittering among the academic staff about my living with Deirdre Amsden. In the Swinging Sixties our association would hardly have twitched an eyebrow, but we were still back in the shame-ridden Fifties, when appearances were deemed all-important. I was made aware, from levels above Hogarth's, that the fornication had to cease lest it spread epidemic-like through the college. So we headed the problem off at the pass one lunchtime by going out and getting married. Fluck gave us a packet of twenty Senior Service as a wedding present, which showed great thoughtfulness as far as I was concerned, as Deirdre did not smoke.

Then there was the matter of the Anti-Ball which Fletcher and I staged in a demure village called Little Shelford just outside Cambridge. We got this house, one of Fletcher's due for renovation, and did up its walls with lurid graphics naming all the destructive influences in the land – from King's College to the monarchy. We then issued invitations for a CND fund-raiser to every activist in the country. It was without question the greatest party in Little Shelford's entire history, but the cops still came to break it up. The whole enterprise was thought to reflect poorly on art students in general, and on the Cambridge school in particular.

I was on probation, obliged to give assurances of improved behaviour, though not for long. I was well into my final year, researching George Grosz's *Ecce Homo* series of drawings for my thesis. But certain things had changed. For one thing conscription had been abolished, so there was no chance of my being immediately presented with the Queen's Shilling on leaving college. For another, I had built up enough contacts, principally through Fletcher and Peter Cook, to give me some assurance of finding work. As it happened, I had to go up to London to do some research for my thesis at the British Museum. I went, and never came back.

CHAPTER FOUR

PORTRAIT OF THE ARTIST
AS A YOUNG YOB

For my advance on London I wore my Cuban-heeled boots which elevated me to a shade under 6 foot 7 inches. My other accoutrements became a lime-green silk shirt with flounces and a grey herringbone-weave suit with silver buttons, flared trousers and trumpet sleeves. I may have been a shade florid, but I was eager to make an impression.

There are a number of theories about the effect of great height on personality, but none, I think, is wholly satisfactory. Perhaps the most informed exchange on the subject was that between the liberal economist John Kenneth Galbraith and General Charles de Gaulle, both men in the 6 foot 8 inches league. On the occasion of their first meeting de Gaulle asked Galbraith to explain his theory of height, to which the

economist replied that very tall people, feeling very conspicuous from an early age, were usually better behaved than their
peers and for that reason better fitted for leadership in later life.
De Gaulle, though evidently pleased with this reply, said that
Galbraith had forgotten just one thing: 'Show no mercy to
small men.'

Perhaps because they have a few inches on me, I have been inclined to see the matter differently. It always seemed to me that if you are going to be conspicuous regardless of what you do, you might as well enjoy the phenomenon by being very conspicuous. At the same time, I've never found it particularly advisable to be merciless to small men, as they are often the ones most likely to give you paying work.

One of the first people in London to take my work seriously was a very small man called Tom Wolsey, then the art director of *Queen* magazine. In those days he held the unofficial title of England's Best Magazine Designer, though he was born in Aachen. Apart from being small he was abrupt and inclined to be waspish, but he gave me a start with a few freelance illustration assignments.

As an introduction to the more surreal end of the communications world, *Queen* in those days could hardly be excelled. Though relatively small in circulation, it was an advertising Klondike with a readership once described as 'the fresh upper crust – crumbs held together by a lot of dough'. But between the glossy motoring ads it managed to insert some very good journalism. The boss and Editor-in-Chief was Jocelyn Stevens, an outstandingly insensitive and energetic young man who had already been highly praised by Lord Beaverbrook, the grand old man of the popular press. Beaverbrook had told a party of dinner guests, 'I hear that Jocelyn Stevens bites the carpet. Now that's no bad thing.'

In fact Stevens used to bite a lot more than carpet. The atmosphere in the *Queen* office often verged on hysteria, as Stevens raged over the Tannoy system. Debby ladies were always leaving in floods of tears, to be replaced by new debby ladies, presumably attracted by the prospect of saying over the phone,

'This is the Queen speaking.' When firing his fashion editor, Stevens affirmed the finality of her departure by hurling her four-drawer filing cabinet out the window, from three floors up.

One of my assignments was to illustrate a feature article about 'The New Rich'. I had assembled a wide range of sensitive studies of stockbrokers, bookmakers, estate agents, auctioneers, barristers and the like, and these were laid out for inspection on the art room floor. Stevens came lunging in and, with extraordinary precision, managed to imprint a boot mark on every single drawing. You can do wonders with fresh bread to efface marks of this kind, but not complete miracles. The drawings went to press with traces of the proprietor's feet still lingering.

It did not seem likely that *Queen* would be a steady enough enterprise to support me and a heavily pregnant Deirdre, even in the gypsy manner to which we had become accustomed. For the time being we were pleasantly holed up in one of Richard Fletcher's renovation projects in Drayton Gardens, Kensington, but things became a bit cramped when a load of other mates from college came piling in. As we could pay most of the rent by illustrating Fletcher's diatribes against the Labour right wing, it was all very much like old times. But it was not the kind of place, at least from our parents' point of view, for bringing up baby.

As an adult, there was a possibility that I might qualify for a student grant, a more generous subvention in those days than it is now, and if I could combine that with some freelance work our circumstances could improve. Ed Middleditch, one of my tutors at the Cambridge school, had urged me to go on to the Royal College of Art. Middleditch was a strange, tortured man of the post-war Kitchen Sink school of painters. At college he had me drawing galvanized tin buckets against a white background for what seemed like decades. Never party to the fashionable enthusiasms, Middleditch tried to impress upon me the need for a high seriousness in my approach to art. He was kind enough to fix up my interview at the Royal College, even though he had reservations about my 'seriousness': 'You have the talent to do more than facile knitting, but I don't suppose you'll be able to help yourself.' A couple of years later I saw an exhibition by Middleditch at the Beaux Arts gallery – powerful charcoal drawings of the wild mountain landscapes of Grazalema in southern Spain. It was the only time an exhibition of drawings moved me to tears, and rather belatedly I got the point.

I did go to the print department of the Royal College to show my work. I could tell that academically the place had much to be said for it, because while I was waiting I fell into the company of a vague-looking young student with a most striking piece of work on a zinc plate entitled 'Me and My Heroes'. It would later feature in all the reference books as David Hockney's first etching. My interview with the print-making tutor Julian Trevelyan went very well, and he asked me to start the next day. I was absolutely thrilled to be accepted by the Royal College, but even as I was confirming the time I should show up I felt all the enthusiasm for actually going there draining away. I never did show up.

I think I had stumbled on the difference between an aspiration and an ambition. I genuinely did aspire to the Royal College, but my ambition, an altogether more red-blooded creature, was to get my work into the newspapers. And, as it happened, the circumstances for realizing this ambition suddenly became highly propitious.

By late 1961 the beginnings of boom time for satire had

arrived. From its high point in 1959, with the 'You've never had it so good' election, the Macmillan era was on the slide. It was clear that Harold Macmillan, the once accomplished old showman, was losing his touch, and the tittering in the aisles had swelled to a chorus of mockery. A revue called *Beyond the Fringe*, in which Peter Cook featured prominently, was en route for the West End where it would provide inspiration for the BBC programme *That Was the Week That Was* (later *TW3*), with David Frost as its anchor man. *Private Eye* opened for business in feisty fashion and, although it would fall on hard times, Peter Cook would alleviate them by buying it up. Another Peter Cook venture was the Establishment Club in Soho, billed as London's first satirical nightclub. Cook's partner in the club was Nicholas Luard, another recent Cambridge graduate. As co-owners of the Establishment they become known as Peter 'Crook' and Nicholas 'Lewd'.

Knowing Peter Cook may not have been the only qualification for advancement in the satire business, but it was certainly no drawback. By the end of the year I was very agreeably employed as the official artist to the Establishment, responsible for filling a 14 foot by 18 inch space opposite the bar every week with a succession of monstrous ideas. Some had religious themes, like St Francis of Assisi being devoured by crows. But most were political. One of my favourites was of Sir Roy Welensky, then the Prime Minister of Southern Rhodesia, and a hero to that strange type of British person, happily more prevalent then than now, who used to rage on about the country being overrun by blacks before announcing that they were off to Africa to be among an infinitely larger number of blacks. For seven days I had Welensky, depicted literally as 'Going the Whole Hog', driving the customers to drink.

The club achieved its greatest notoriety when the American comedian Lenny Bruce appeared there spraying four-letter words like confetti, which failed to conceal the fact that he was a very funny man. On one occasion a famous actress, accompanied by an early version of the toyboy, gave him a hard time, so Bruce invited her to leave, and take her son with her.

One club regular was my old friend Tom Driberg, the left-wing Labour MP, suspected at various times of working for every secret service outfit on the planet from MI5 to the KGB, and known to be the most voracious homosexual in British politics. I had first met Driberg at the Scarborough conference in 1960 at one of those hotel functions that let the agitators in. We got on famously, though I was not entirely unaware of the reasons for Driberg's interest in me. Nor, it appeared, was Barbara Castle, who happened to notice there was a handbag left on a chair behind where I was standing. She picked it up, turned to me with the sweetest smile, and said, 'Is this yours, dear?'

As it turned out, Driberg became a very good friend to both Fluck and myself without being granted any sexual favours. We used to say that the great thing about him was that he was so corrupt he was completely incorruptible. In any event, he would supply me with a never-ending stream of funny ideas for my space on the wall. I even had some left over to decorate the walls of another club called Wip's in which Nicholas Luard had an interest. I remember the competition for attention being particularly fierce there as each table was imaginatively equipped with a glass tank in which piranhas swam around, ever ready to help the diners with their leftovers.

There were certain penalties to pay for the Driberg friendship. It was impossible of course to go anywhere with him without it being assumed that you were his boyfriend. But I

always thought this was a very modest price to pay for the pleasure of his company. However, I would start to pay a bigger price, particularly when Driberg came to look to me for companionship when he ventured into places that made him slightly apprehensive. I was often in demand when he went down to the East End at the invitation of his gangster mates, the twins Ronald and Reginald Kray. I can remember the first time very well as the twins thoughtfully came round to the House of Commons in a Rolls-Royce to pick up Driberg and myself. We were installed in the back seat with our hosts and the man next to the driver turned to me and said, in deepest guttural Cockney, 'Would you like a scar?' Luckily, Driberg was able to translate the threat as a friendly offer of a cigar.

These events in the East End were jolly but more than slightly unnerving. There would be a lot of sports and showbiz people being encouraged by the Krays to have a good time. So a good time was a smart thing to have. Around the twins themselves there was an extraordinary air of impending violence, and of course, as the lurid details of their trial would eventually reveal, there were many individuals against whom the violence did not merely impend. But with Driberg they were models of solicitude. There would always be a young man, usually of a slightly effeminate nature, assigned to keep him entertained. The tragedy of it was that Driberg never did manage to summon up the nerve to tell the Krays that he did not much care for effeminate men. He liked lorry drivers and policemen, the hunkier the better.

I also became friendly with one of the Krays' enforcers called Teddy Smith who had literary ambitions, and who acted as part-time crime adviser for BBC's *Softly, Softly* cops-and-robbers series. I once asked him whether, as part of his day job, he

46

had ever shot people for the Krays. 'Naw, Rog,' he said, 'only through the kneecaps.' He was hoping to obtain a sabbatical from the Kray firm which would give him time to finish his musical, provisionally entitled *Cosh*, but there was some kind of disagreement and Teddy Smith disappeared totally from the scene. Many years later I had occasion to visit Reggie Kray in prison while in pursuit of an authentic quote to promote a sketch I was developing about two puppet gangsters called 'The Crows'. We drank vodka together out of the Coke tins I had taken in to lighten the occasion. Emboldened by the vodka, I inquired about what had happened to my mate Teddy Smith. 'I fink he emigrated to Australia,' was the terse reply.

In the summer of 1962 the *Observer* gave its grave accolade to satire by a establishing a new page imaginatively called 'Satire' to differentiate it from the rest of the product. Peter Cook and Michael Frayn were the main writers, while Cook and I produced a running cartoon strip under the prophetic title 'Almost the End'. My first cartoon strip in a national newspaper was directed at a brace of soft targets, Hugh Gaitskell and George Brown. We had a frazzled-looking Labour leader imploring his hard-eyed henchman to stop calling him 'Brother' because, 'it reminds me so much of the Labour Party'. After such a modest start, the *Observer* was convinced we were bound to improve. And we did, quite rapidly. It was not long before Cook produced his deathless critical observation: 'I go to the theatre to be entertained. I don't want to see plays about rape, sodomy and drug addiction – I can get all that at home.'

The progress of the new satire page was keenly watched by the *Observer*'s patrician editor, David Astor, though most of my practical dealings were with George Seddon, one of the livelier executives. On the strength of Seddon's commission, Deirdre and I moved to a flat of our own in Peter Street, Soho, with baby Shem. To judge by the nature of the surrounding establishments we would not have to waste much time teaching him the facts of life.

My orderly progress into journalism nearly came unstuck with the Cuban missile crisis. For a few weeks in October, as the Russians and the Americans played their lunatic game of nuclear 'chicken', there was virtual mob rule in parts of the West End of London. What were conceived as orderly demonstrations soon degenerated into free-for-alls. There were reports of extreme hotheads going around torching police motorcycles, which I knew to be true as I set one alight myself. More perilously, I got involved outside the American Embassy when two youngsters darted into the street to stop a police wagon. A police sergeant got out and really laid into these two kids, so I laid into the police sergeant and knocked him down. Then a load of other policemen came piling out of the wagon, tripping over one another like Keystone Cops. I must have clumped another four of them before I legged it down the street. They caught me and took me to Cannon Row police station, by which time I was blubbing on a grand scale. Assault and battery of five police officers was not going to be just another £5 fine coupled with an admonishment to behave in future. But the police were in a funny mood, not just about the incident, which arguably they had started, but about the whole situation. I realized with some surprise, though it should have been obvious, that the cops were as scared about the nuclear showdown as anyone else and that, on one level at least, they were glad that people were demonstrating against it. I blubbed on for a couple of hours before they decided to drop the assault charges and do me for rioting, which then carried a nominal fine. At the court hearing I saw one of the policemen, all strapped up. 'You bastard,' he said. 'If I'd known what you'd done to me I wouldn't have dropped the charges. You've cracked two of my ribs.' But their leniency, if regretted, was not entirely misplaced. For the first time in my relations with the police I felt I seriously owed them one. I never waded into them with the same relish again.

This was not quite the end of my fighting days, however. In fact I was involved in a major brawl only a few weeks later with one of the rather unsavoury heavies that were infiltrating the Establishment Club in increasing numbers. Ostensibly I got the better of it but when I got home Deirdre said, 'What's happened to your coat?' I took the coat off and it was like a Chinese lantern, with long slashes all down the front. I had never even realized my opponent had a razor. I had just learned another important lesson, which was that London brawlers have much less respect for the Queensberry Rules than their country cousins in Cambridgeshire. Not long after I was told that some large men in Italian suits had dropped by at the club looking for me. I was advised to send in my cartoon strip by post.

What with one thing and another, pastures new were beginning to look more and more appealing. Neither my satirical drawings nor my direct action in Grosvenor Square had made much impression on the Government. Nuclear weapons, it appeared, were here to stay despite my best efforts. Meanwhile life on the *Observer* was proving to have limitations, best expressed by its deputy editor, John Pringle, who had previously been editor of the *Sydney Morning Herald*. Pringle explained that while Leon Trotsky had invented the permanent revolution, it was the *Observer* which had invented the permanent deliberation, an ongoing angst-ridden seminar that often had little relevance to what appeared in the newspaper. It had its charm, but Pringle felt there was more excitement to be had elsewhere, which was why he was heading back to Australia to edit the *Canberra Times*. He thought he could probably find work for me on one of the magazines out there.

I was within a whisker of emigration until I stumbled upon a forceful counter-argument. This, somewhat paradoxically, was provided by a cultural official at the Australian Embassy. By way of introduction to the mores of his country he showed me a film of Australian shipbuilders wearing shorts and asbestos gloves catching white hot rivets and exhibiting quite a lot of what I was brought up to call builder's bum. I explained that I had nothing against dockyards, but my preference was to work on a magazine. The embassy man slumped back aghast into his chair. 'Christ, have you seen our magazines?' he exclaimed. He then handed me some copies, which did look a bit old-fashioned, before imparting the clinching advice, 'Look, mate, it took me years to get this job in London. Believe me, going to Australia is a one-way ticket to hell.' On the strength of what seemed like top-quality inside information I put the Australian experience on hold for quite a while.

CHAPTER FIVE

THE SIXTIES

Swinging London, so revered in retrospect, was very slow getting into its stride. My own memories of the capital in the early sixties are all monochrome, like the gritty black and white films of the period. Around Fleet Street and St Paul's Cathedral there was still a profusion of bombsites and half-destroyed buildings, deep in weeds. The city, and most of its citizens, looked decidedly glum.

Eating out for sophisticates not content with fish and chips usually boiled down to a coin-tossing choice between the Golden Egg chain or a Lyons Corner House. The pubs all seemed dowdy and to be woefully devoid of any beer not called Watney's Red Barrel. Only the locality known as Soho seemed to offer much in the way of variety, which was its main attraction for me.

In Soho there was a sprinkling of Italian restaurants that at least gave bored taste buds something different to think about. The most popular of these was the Terrazza in Romilly Street where Mario and Franco served Cocktail di Mare followed by Pollo Sorpreso, a sort of Chicken Kiev with a genuine element of surprise. However the dish was tackled, liquid butter always exploded down the front of your shirt. The pasta washed down with libations of vino tinto was popular with young journalists as it did not hurt on the way back up.

Pubs closed early, and during the afternoons, but in Soho you could still drink practically round the clock. The trail blazed by thirsty bohemians of the Francis Bacon and Dylan Thomas variety tended to start at the York Minister pub, better known as the French, in Dean Street, and then lead on to the Colony Room, an easy access club with an afternoon licence, and then on to any other pub of choice before the serious after-hours drinking. This could take place at the Establishment Club in Greek Street. At the Establishment, however, you had to purchase a meal with your drink, so you could easily wind up with a dozen sad-looking, uneaten hamburgers mouldering at your elbow. A better option, especially for music lovers, was Ronnie Scott's jazz club. Scott had somehow managed to persuade the licensing authorities that drinks could be served in the event of a legitimate birthday celebration. Visiting musicians like Stan Getz would leave Ronnie Scott's decades older, having had a birthday on every night of their gigs.

At break of day, anyone managing to complete the course could find further refreshment by posing as a meat porter, and frequenting one of the pubs open for their use in Smithfield Market. Looking back, it's hard to figure out how we ever found the time to earn a crust.

For a short spell my earning power was threatened, not by drink but by a sobering assessment of one of my 'Almost the End' cartoon efforts for the *Observer*. The inspiration was provided by a news story about a man being birched in prison. I illustrated this theme by having the then Home Secretary, Rab Butler, discussing flogging with his lady wife in an English country garden while lopping the heads off tulips with his stick. This brought my work to the direct attention of the Editor. David Astor told me that he rather liked the tulip-chopping image, but he was outraged by the inclusion of the Home Secretary's wife in the joke. He told me that in attacking public figures I had to learn how to distinguish between the public and private in their lives, but I never did. It was curtains for the 'Almost the End' strip but Astor, being an exceptionally humane man, allowed me to stay on. I was put on a two-day-a-week retainer and allocated a tiny attic office on the Tudor Street premises. From this pleasant niche I launched a vigorous assault on the freelance market, though, out of consideration for my kindly employer, I would only do work for his main rival publication, the *Sunday Times*, under an assumed name.

There was still plenty of work to be done for *Queen*, though my original patron Tom Wolsey had been let go by Jocelyn Stevens with characteristic panache. Stevens had rushed into Wolsey's vacated office and set about it with bucket and mop while muttering incantations about washing that man right out of his hair. Wolsey, of course, was far too talented to remain on the cobbles for very long and he bounced back almost immediately as the art editor of *Town*, another attractive glossy of the day. So I worked for *Queen* and *Town* and when *Town* acquired a stablemate called *Topic*, a doomed attempt to produce a British *Newsweek*, I worked for that too.

For a while *Town* was edited by Nick Tomalin, a superb young writer who would eventually be killed while covering the Yom Kippur War for the *Sunday Times*. But what impressed me about Tomalin at the time was not his writing skill so much as his ability to inflame Wolsey. I remember walking in on a blazing row between them over some design problem in which Wolsey expressed his artistic dissent by removing Tomalin's hat and coat from the coat stand, placing them carefully on the floor, and jumping up and down on them.

Until 1964 there were no colour supplements in the newspapers aside from the *Sunday Times*, and even that was struggling to master the technique of printing back-to-back colour. So the established independent colour magazines like *Queen* and *Town* were really quite influential. Of the two I tended to prefer *Town*, which was part of the Haymarket Press combine owned by two rising young thrusters called Michael Heseltine and Clive Labovitch (more popularly known as 'Vaseline' and 'Lavatory Brush'). The main part of the empire was devoted to business magazines produced by hordes of young journalists in conditions that would give a battery hen claustrophobia. In contrast, *Town* was an indulged area, though a shrinking one. It had originally been called *Man About Town*, which subsequently became *About Town*, so after the foreshortening to *Town* it really had no place to go. But before it died it made some forays into serious journalism and I was able to brush up my 'artist reporting' skills on subjects slightly less frivolous than those that came my way from *Queen*.

My most serious assignment, however, came from the current affairs magazine, *Topic*, which asked me to do a cover showing what life, or the lack of it, would be like after a nuclear holocaust.

None of this freelance activity required neglect of my duties at the *Observer*, as these were not onerous. Having established to David Astor's satisfaction that I was not to be trusted in the official mockery squad, I tended to be deployed on pure illustration work, doing the drawings for other people's articles. As most of the other people were interesting, this was usually agreeable work. The place was full of wise older brothers and uncles who could tell you any number of things you didn't know, and it was not entirely deficient in a pleasant class of young tearaway. One of the nicest of them, a youngster from Finsbury Park called Don McCullin, was already on the road to becoming the world's greatest war photographer since Robert Capa.

My own outdoor assignments were, happily, less dangerous but not without their perils. Many of these occurred in association with Jeremy Sandford, an upper-class writer absorbed by what he saw as working-class culture. Sandford later wrote an excellent television play about homelessness called *Cathy Come Home*, but during my spell with him he was more concerned with workers at play. Thus I would find myself marooned in fun-loving places like Clacton-on-Sea and Majorca, eternally waiting for Sandford to show up.

My worst experience was at a Butlin's camp, quartered with the young folk. There was a terrible outbreak of 'chalet rash' – the camp name for love bites. The noise of after-dark activity got so intense that, after four sleepless nights, I begged to be relocated with the old age pensioners. Next morning Sandford bounced in full of beans and bouquets for the culture – 'I do love the plastic parrots here, don't you, Roger? You must have been having the most wonderful time.' I refrained from throttling him. Sandford's journeys through the working-class at play were subsequently reproduced in book form, with my drawings as illustrations. I don't think it a pinnacle of achievement for either of us, but the title wasn't bad. It was called *Synthetic Fun*.

My work on the *Observer* helped me to evolve techniques that best suited my skill. Pencil drawings in newspaper illustrations were almost invariably reproduced in half-tone blocks, and very nondescript they could look too. To get round this I would draw on very thin layout paper spread over a thick cartridge paper with a strong grain in it, and this would give the effect of a broken line, perfect for reproduction for the much blacker line blocks. I also did woodcuts which really took advantage of the line block. One of my woodcuts printed on page 1 of the *Observer* could clearly be seen in reverse on page 2. I was a long way from being the best draughtsman in the newspaper business but I liked to think that nobody else could make their stuff leap so far off the page.

The most significant political event during my time at the *Observer* was the election in 1964 of a new Labour government. This was a body blow for satire, which had gorged itself on the Profumo Affair and Tory decline. There was a feeling, even on the far left, that with a new dawn of political wisdom satire would no longer be necessary. I did not share the optimism on this point, because there was something that troubled me about Harold Wilson. I couldn't help it. I just didn't like his face. In those days I thought it possible that I was being unfair, but I later discovered a powerful precedent for this form of political analysis. While the American Civil War was raging, Abraham Lincoln rejected an excellently qualified ministerial candidate on the grounds that he did not like his face. When reproved by his aides for vetoing an appointment on such flimsy grounds,

Lincoln observed: 'Every man over forty is responsible for his own face.'

As the *Observer* was easily the most liberal of the quality Sunday newspapers, it might be thought that it would be the one most energized by the election of a Labour government. This did not prove to be the case. Things puttered on in the old paternalistic way. It was said that there was no human foible that the editor could not understand, so if I managed to stay out of jail I was confronted with the daunting possibility of a job for life.

The sense of security would probably have been less oppressive had it not been for the fact that the *Sunday Times*, once considered a tired old Tory rag, was acquiring a wildly exciting reputation. Its by now stylish colour magazine easily eclipsed the clumsy new productions of the *Observer* and *Sunday Telegraph*, while its news section was becoming famous for something called 'the beer bottle school of journalism', which would write, edit and design right through Friday night in order to trounce the opposition. Within the scholastic portals of the *Observer* all this frantic activity in the enemy camp was rather frowned upon, but the young hopefuls on the payroll all started to twitch.

Peter Dunn, the *Observer*'s best young reporter, was the first to defect, and he was followed, after a short interval, by Don McCullin and myself. I was enticed to the *Sunday Times* by Michael Rand, the art editor of its colour magazine, who was already known to me as a man of considerable resources. For one thing he had reached his level of visual eminence with only one functioning eye; for another, he had been responsible for the famous 'Expressograph' feature when he worked with the *Daily Express*, then reckoned the most innovative of the popular newspapers, and undoubtedly the most imaginative. Rand's 'Expressograph' was a skilled compilation of graphs and diagrams which helped persuade the readers of a number of comforting patriotic propositions about the solidity of their Empire, how the British nuclear deterrent was superior to the American one, and so on. At my recruitment interview, a gruelling three-hour lunch at the Terrazza, Rand made it clear to me that I, too, should be flexible. I was to work for both the newspaper and the magazine, and I had to be ready to draw anything from a sampan to a sausage in five minutes flat.

The *Sunday Times* had a very strong team of news photographers, but there were certain areas that they could not reach or felt disinclined to venture. So I would get to do the news drawings for things like Chinese gambling dens, where the photographers were likely to get their cameras smashed, and big courtroom scenes, where cameramen were not allowed to take pictures. As it happens, drawing was not allowed either, but you could make a fair stab at it by going along and making a few doodles in your pocket and doing the composition from memory later.

On one of these jobs I was allowed to penetrate behind the scenes at the Old Bailey, where I was fascinated to discover a system of light switches as intricate as anything you might find backstage at a Drury Lane theatre. Behind the majesty of the law scrupulous attention was paid to special effects. I was naturally a critic of all the flummery and pedantry of courtroom proceedings, though much less so after I had been sent to draw Myra Hindley and Ian Brady at the Moors Murder trial. On that occasion I was grateful for the artificiality of it all, as a means of taking the edge off the horror under discussion.

I got to know the top brass at the *Sunday Times* quite quickly, less through my own efforts than because I shared an office with David Hillman, a fantastically meticulous young designer who used to do the 'Review Front', the main features showcase of the newspaper that was always vetted at the top level. Hardly a week would go by without Hillman hammering the desk with his metal rule and threatening to resign over how insensitive journalists were butchering his magnificent constructions. I would have to pad along the corridors of power seeking compromise solutions.

Most of my real work was done for the magazine, where my immediate boss was David King, the associate art editor and the real designing genius of the enterprise. King was just 22, a year younger than myself, and unusual in a number of respects. He had an unnerving cackling laugh and spoke with a wheezy Cockney intonation that suggested three lifetimes spent on sixty gaspers a day. Strangers would invariably find him disconcerting. Once, when King was hospitalized after a serious car accident, a doctor told his wife, Philomena, that she should brace herself for a shock when seeing him as it was unlikely that he would ever be the same man again. After seeing her husband, Mrs King was able to comfort the doctor with the reassurance that her husband had always been like that.

On any magazine the relationship between the illustrator and the designer is crucial to its appearance, and mine with King was already good. On emerging from the London College of Printing as the hotshot typographer of his generation, King had done postgraduate studies in obstreperous behaviour by working closely with Tom Wolsey at both *Queen* and *Town*. He had even flashed through at the *Observer* but left after a few weeks, raging at 'duffle coat designers' who didn't know a headline from a hole in the wall. King's judgements were of a quite astonishing rapidity and for the most part astonishingly acute, though they were assisted by his ability to dismiss vast acres of artistic experience as 'boring'. He believed that Mark Rothko was the greatest artist since Rembrandt, and possibly before that. I remember one distinguished illustrator, who had shown King his work, making a loud moan about its being dismissed 'in five minutes'. When King was later reproached for being so abrupt, he also took offence: 'Five minutes, never. It didn't take ten seconds.'

King had hung around the *Observer* just long enough for us to establish an informal freelance partnership, a sort of business within a business, available to clients keen to draw attention to themselves. We did an issue of *Vogue* together, but our most interesting association, prior to the *Sunday Times*, had been on *Magnet News*, billed as Britain's first black newspaper, for which King devised the biggest logo in creation. The launch was announced from the Commonwealth Institute where we met Malcolm X, the American black militant leader, and I could not help noticing that for a man fond of describing white people as 'blue-eyed devils' he had an interesting facial feature – very blue eyes. King and I had lot of fun putting the newspaper together, but after the first issue they let the white men go. Shortly afterwards they let everybody go. But it was the bold design of *Magnet News* that first led Michael Rand and Mark Boxer, the magazine's editor, to suspect that we might have something to offer the *Sunday Times*.

King's mandate on the magazine was to make it look livelier – a golden opportunity for a man who wanted to smuggle pop newspaper, and later pop art, techniques into the quality press – and a lot more colourful, which was partly where I came in. One of the major problems of the early magazine was that, while it had access to many exciting new colour processes through its press in Watford, most of the best stories would still come in as black and white. This was partly because all the best stock pictures were monochrome and partly because some of the very best photographers, Don McCullin being a prime example, were averse to shooting in colour. As a counterbalance to this, King thought the magazine should inject much more colour into its illustrations. Since I had developed a line in garish woodcuts – more specifically, hardboard cuts – along with my drawing, I was well fitted to assist in this cause. The brash background colour for these works could be effortlessly inserted in the form of instructions to the printer.

King made a point of getting to know the potential of the technology at Watford, and as a result he soon began to come up with ideas for beefing up the appearance of photo-stories that still had to be in black and white. He started introducing four-colour black into the magazine, which would give pictures much greater depth on the page. It was a highly expensive improvement but, as King was fond of pointing out, spending the proprietor's money to keep the *Observer* and *Telegraph* thrashing about in our wake was doing him an enormous favour.

Without realizing my luck, I had moved from boom time for satire to boom time for the newspaper business. Looking back, it is apparent that the mid-sixties period of the *Sunday Times* was the most creative phase in newspapers since the war. This was the time when the Insight column was born, and when it was at its best, breaking and remaking every traditional rule about how a quality paper should look. Other newspapers were obliged to pay it the compliment of aping its methods. It seemed as if a general advance in the freedom and authority of the press was being made. It was only later that we realized this was a freak occurrence.

Perhaps the most freakish aspect of the newspaper in those days was having a proprietor who did not interfere. Though no moral giant, Lord Thomson knew how to delegate. The other peculiarity was the age range. Aside from a thin layer of avuncular figures who had been in submarines and Spitfires in the war and were located at the very top, it was hard to find anybody there over 35. Indeed, most of the high-pressure jobs in the newsroom and departments like Insight were done by people in their twenties. This was partly a by-product of expansion, but it was also the consequence of a deliberate hiring policy. On the *Sunday Times* this alliance between the war generation and the new generation was a key source of energy, and I suspect it was the main factor behind many other areas of sixties creativity. While a lot of youths were having their way, there were also some shrewd old buzzards allowing them to have it. The shrewdest of them all was Denis Hamilton, an editor of almost painful reticence who had served on Montgomery's staff during the war. Hamilton was succeeded by Harry Evans, a more charismatic figure, and newspaper histories tend to give Evans most credit for the emergence of the *Sunday Times* as a great newspaper. But he only drove the engine, albeit brilliantly. It was Hamilton who built it.

Another stroke of luck from my point of view was that I was getting the best that Australian journalism had to offer without actually going there. Among expatriate Australian wordsmiths in London the *Sunday Times* was known as 'the lifeboat'. Bruce Page, London born but Melbourne raised, was the first on board, and very soon afterwards set about hauling on his Aussie mates, in roughly chronological order Phillip Knightley,

Murray Sayle, Tony Clifton, Alex Mitchell and Nelson Mews. All of them were excellent journalists – Sayle and Knightley became award-winning feature writers, while Page was the true genius of the Insight operation – but what appealed to me most was their lively sense of mockery about practically everything, not excluding themselves.

Sayle, the philosopher of the group, had written a novel called *A Crooked Sixpence* about his earlier days as a reporter on the downmarket *People* newspaper. The book had been withdrawn for libel reasons, but its well-thumbed proofs did the rounds of journalists samizdat-style. I can remember the eloquent frontispiece:

> *There was a crooked man*
> *Who walked a crooked mile*
> *He found a crooked sixpence*
> *And it wasn't enough*

I became, and remained, good friends with most of these agreeable Aussie characters. Indeed, I began to form a rose-tinted view of the country that produced them. Then the Australian newspaper proprietor in the shape of Rupert Murdoch, the Dirty Digger, arrived, and balanced the picture.

Although the *Sunday Times* generated a lot of bustle, there were certain still centres. One of them was Godfrey Smith, who succeeded Mark Boxer as editor of the magazine, and who probably delegated even more efficiently than Lord Thomson. Most of the magazine's ideas emerged from a 'think tank' he set up and which usually consisted of Rand, King, the writer Francis Wyndham and the fashion editor Meriel McCooey. In consequence, Smith was able to sit serenely behind a desk without a single scrap of paper on it. If, however, you had to go and see his deputy, you had to take a machete to the stacked files in his office to get at him. Even so, Smith was more than a diplomat. Whenever a difficult decision came up, like whether Don McCullin's brilliant but harrowing pictures from Vietnam should be allowed to spoil the reader's breakfast, he almost invariably came down on the side of the radicals.

One of my first major jobs for Smith was a series of drawings for Graham Greene's novel *The Comedians*, which was serialized in the magazine. They were done in sombre shades of green, brown and grey, and had a certain delicacy of touch, to my mind. They also managed to catch the attention of a reviewer in the journal of the Hornsey School of Art, where I had done some teaching in my loafing days at the *Observer*. 'I feel,' said the reviewer, 'that Roger Law has extended himself beyond his resources, rather like someone trying to play Wagner on a Jew's harp.'

Among writers on the magazine, the one we found most stimulating was Bruce Chatwin, who had done a runner from Sotheby's to become a travel writer. Chatwin's returns to home base were always good value. I can remember him, ice-blue eyes blazing, declaiming the works of the Russian poet, Osip Mandelstam, to a spellbound art department. Hard to imagine such impromptu cultural events happening today in Rupert Murdoch's *Sunday Times*.

Critics these days maintain that Chatwin embroidered his exotica, and it is possible that he did not always allow the facts to impede the delivery of a good story. However, his perceptions were often way ahead of the conventional wisdom. At a time when the polarities in the Cold War seemed wholly immutable, I can remember Chatwin explaining to me that

Muslim aspirations in the Soviet Union would eventually lead to a solid defensive alliance between the Kremlin, representing the Russian people, and the West.

David King and Chatwin were yoked together by their mutual interest in the Soviet Union. King at the time was like one of Chekhov's three sisters, always exclaiming, 'I want to go to Moscow.' Eventually he got his wish, and he and Chatwin visited Mandelstam's widow there. I have always had a suspicion that Chatwin's book *Utz* (about a fixated collector of Meissen porcelain) was based on King's obsessively accumulated collection of photographs of the Russian revolution and its aftermath.

At the *Sunday Times*, as on the *Observer*, King and I managed to keep a sideline going. With the onset of crushed velvet bell-bottom trousers and ever tinier mini skirts, and the general brightening up into the sixties as they are now remembered, this incidental work became more interesting. Our most popular success occurred when Chris Stamp of Track Records commissioned us to do a couple of record covers – one for Jimi Hendrix, and another for The Who.

Hendrix, exhibiting London's first Afro and a braided jacket emblazoned with the words 'Don't Stare', was easy to work with, and one of the images we created with him became the best-selling poster of the decade. Indeed, our design for his album *Axis Bold as Love* can still be seen gracing the CD to this day. The Who assignment posed more intricate problems of persuasion. Our concept required Pete Townshend to apply a three-foot replica of a deodorant roll-on to his armpit, while Roger Daltrey was invited to immerse himself in a bath of cold Heinz baked beans to achieve the desired artistic effect. The photo shoot went well enough, but Townshend's exposed armpit

Jimi Hendrix

got the album banned from stores in the United States. There was no significant objection to Daltrey's bathing in Heinz beans, except from the singer himself who developed pneumonia.

I enjoyed these diversions from mainstream journalism without seeing them as a serious alternative to the real thing. But at the same time my conception of the real thing was changing. Without being in any way dissatisfied with the paper, I knew there would be no repetition of the great days of 'artist reporting' as defined by Paul Hogarth. In the modern world it could only start where photography left off, and photography could now go practically everywhere. Illustration might still be important to a newspaper's overall appearance, but it was not something you found people discussing in pubs, unless they happened to be other illustrators. There was still a place for great draughtsmanship, of course, like that evinced by two contemporaries of mine, Gerald Scarfe and Ralph Steadman, but I was never going to be able to draw as well as those guys. If I was ever going to excite the regulars in the Pig and Whistle, I would have to come up with something else.

Peter Fluck and I had discussed the possibility of model-making for profit at college but, as there did not seem to be any demand, nothing got made. Later I can remember being impressed by some 3-D figures produced by Ed Kienholtz and exhibited at the Institute of Contemporary Arts (ICA). In one tableau a life-sized couple embraced on a bed. If you took the trouble to look into their ears you could see images inside their heads. They were both fantasizing, but clearly not about each other. Although the modelling of the figures was fairly rough, it seemed to me that Kienholtz had come up with a concept that was capable of development.

Then in the summer of 1966 a small window of journalistic

opportunity swung open. *Nova*, which was one of the livelier magazines around, asked me to illustrate a feature about Catholicism with something a bit different. So I modelled a priest and a penitent in plasticine, and we established communication between them by cutting a hole in intervening the page. The heads were crudely modelled and only adequately photographed, but the effect was novel enough to win a Design and Art Directors' Association award. I did not capitalize on this modest breakthrough with any great speed, because an American adventure intervened.

CHAPTER SIX

STARS AND BARS

Some years ago it was revealed that the Central Intelligence Agency had secretly channelled funds to the various foundations who made a speciality of subsidizing European students and scholars visiting the United States. The thinking behind this was that your average anti-American young lefty from Europe would, on exposure to the United States, be so feeble-minded as to fall in love with the place and become pro-American for ever more. It was a cynical, manipulative policy, but in my case almost wholly effective.

My invitation to take up a teaching post at as artist-in-residence at Reed College in Portland, Oregon, came from James Webb, a member of the faculty there who, in an earlier incarnation, had been one of my editors on *Granta* in Cambridge.

The Rockefeller Foundation then came through with a grant sufficient to support me and my family for six months. We were now, with the birth of Sophie, four in number, but still highly mobile. We had never exactly put down deep roots in London, having lived at five different addresses ranging from Notting Hill Gate to Soho in five years. So another move, even to the far side of the United States, was no major wrench.

I took up my academic duties in the autumn of 1967, when Lyndon Baines Johnson was still President and the country was in turmoil over the war in Vietnam. In the London we had just left, dissent against the war was still very much the preserve of the radical left. Wilson's Labour government, though shrewd enough not to lend any troops to the enterprise, was firmly pro-Johnson on the grounds of having to show loyalty to the Americans. In Oregon there was scarcely a loyal American in sight on the subject of the war, while on the campus at Reed positive hostility tended to prevail.

This partly stemmed from Reed's radical tradition. The institution was founded by the John Reed who wrote *Ten Days that Shook the World*, a celebration of the Bolshevik revolution in Russia. But the more important reason for dismay at the war, not only at Reed but on all the American campuses, was the havoc it was playing with the academic system. Everyone knew that a young man's ejection from college amounted to conscription for a war growing more unpopular by the minute, and in this situation the marking of male students became utterly bizarre. There were a few tutors who did not succumb to the temptation to give high marks to the lowest achievers, but I was not one of them.

The other serious temptation I succumbed to was drugs. Though I deliberately refrained from LSD and sticking needles up my arm, I took full advantage of the wide range of speed and marijuana on offer. I cannot say that the ingestion of these substances actually improved my work, but the amphetamines certainly enabled me to tap sources of energy I had not previously been aware of. However, after one episode when my heart seemed to be making a great effort to leap out of my body, I came to use speed very sparingly. My experiences with marijuana were more benign and led to some interesting encounters.

One of these was with Howard Rheingold, who used to attend campus events dressed as a cockroach. In human form Rheingold had tight blond curls and blackcurrant black eyes which were always fixed on some lunatic proposition. One of his experiments, in which I was very happy to participate, involved getting very seriously stoned. Then, when you were in this condition, Rheingold would couple you up to his machine – an arrangement of wires which would dangle from your head and led to a screen which flashed up your alpha rhythms. As the experiment developed you would have to try to reproduce these same alpha rhythms without the benefit of drugs, and you would do this by learning certain in-brain entertainment techniques. To some extent it could actually be done, but the cumbersome technology prevented wider application. It was always Rheingold's ambition to get the whole thing down to the size of a wristwatch, which would enable him to tap into the market of Wall Street businessmen eager to get stoned on the way to work. We naturally all thought that Rheingold was as mad as a cockroach, but he later surfaced as the editor of the *Whole Earth Catalog*, a highly respected environmental publication, and as the author of best-selling works about advanced computer applications – *The Virtual Community* and *Smart Mobs*.

He also regularly gives evidence on techno-ecological matters to Congressional committees, and is listened to with the utmost respect.

My only official duty at Reed was teaching illustration, but I had a drug-induced notion that it might be fun to make a puppet film with the help of student volunteers and Will Baker, a lecturer from Boise, Idaho, who taught English in a cowboy hat. The basic idea was to construct a little team of marionettes who could act out the life of a family of the future. This family's chief characteristic would be that it had completely come to terms with the consumer society. Everything about them had to be standardized, down to the number of children, which in America at that time was 2.4. We were unable to think of a way of conveying 0.4 of a child, so we compromised by calling our smallest puppet 'Point Four'.

Few other compromises were made. The family subsisted by eating and excreting money. However, all purchases were made by computer. All payments were made by the puppets with their right hands, which had usefully mutated into credit cards. These would be inserted into the slot in the computer. Nobody ever left home, because there was no reason to. They all became very obese. It was hardly Orwell or Huxley as a vision of the future, but we really enjoyed working out some of the ideas. Unfortunately, when it was screened the film was really boring, all too ponderous and hopelessly overlong. I thought then that it was highly unlikely I would ever be able to do anything worthwhile with puppets.

Reed College also provided me with an interesting insight into academic social life, as my special position there introduced me to a round of dinner parties of the no-holds-barred variety celebrated in Edward Albee's *Who's Afraid of Virginia*

Woolf? It was, I began to realize, very difficult for even the largest intellects to rise above the problem of inhabiting a small world. The back-stabbing I encountered in academia far excelled anything I encountered in the genteel fields of print and television.

When our time was up in Oregon, we moved on to San Francisco, where I was confident I could find work on one of the newspapers. While Sophie galloped through our dwindling funds riding the carousel in Golden Gate Park, I sussed out the employment prospects. I liked the gutsy approach of the *Bay Guardian*, but found it was too poor to consider taking me on. The *San Francisco Chronicle* was rich enough but they thought my work was too highly seasoned for their readers' palates. They suggested I try the underground.

At first I thought they meant the subway, but they were only giving me a kindly steer to the underground press which served San Francisco's buoyant 'peace and love' hippie community. I was not at all affronted by this suggestion, but I knew that such publications usually revolved around a little gang of mates, and I would have to develop contacts before I could get in. However, I did have what might be described as a character reference in this area on the strength of my album covers for Jimi Hendrix and The Who. But even with this nothing much transpired beyond the offer of a job on a new magazine devoted to pop music. I was able to pass on this as I could see no possible future in a specialist journal called *Rolling Stone*. Like the man who declined the opportunity to give the Beatles a recording contract, I subsequently thought I might conceivably have made a mistake. Meanwhile the money ran out. Deirdre and I decided that she and the children should return to England for the brief time it would take for me to hit it big in America, and then they would come back again. It was a year before I saw them again.

Paid work, when I found it, was not as exalted as sweeping the subway, but it had its compensations. I was taken on to draw what was known as 'Merch on the Fig' by an in-house fashion agency serving a big department store. No great initiative was required. All you had to do was draw the department store's merchandise on the human figures. But some of the figures were quite extraordinary. As this was San Francisco and I was in the fashion trade, it was naturally assumed that I was gay. So there would be this cavalcade of women, from blackest black to corn-fed white, taking off their clothes and putting on the 'Merch', and vice versa, completely unselfconsciously in front of me. And I'd be trying to do the drawings while sweating bullets at the same time.

The stress of this work was eased by the many opportunities for recreation in concerts at the Phillmore West and sometimes in the park. I got to see the Grateful Dead, Jefferson Airplane and the wonderfully over-the-top Janis Joplin, who so took my fancy that I made a large-scale model of her. This was ultimately unsatisfactory because it could not do justice to her two greatest attributes – her voice, which was great, and her language, which was unbelievably foul.

My politics on the West Coast were catered for by the Peace and Freedom Party, a radical group which was closely allied to the Black Panthers. It was through this connection that I came to attend a number of Panther functions in Oakland, which were really quite extraordinary. When you went in you were given a joint as long as your arm, and from then on it was all about having a ball. At one rally I remember they had a white tambourine girl in the band and she would periodically clap the instrument above her head in a motion that obliged her skirt to rise and reveal pure, all-American pussy. The outrageousness of the Panthers was probably the one issue on which all the police-men and all the feminists in America were totally united.

Yet it was all curiously traditional in its way. I realized that the blacks' macho attitude was really their version of John Wayne, lone man with a gun, reversed out. It was Whitey who invented John Wayne and they were just turning the character around, though they could never bring themselves to dress badly enough to bring the masquerade off completely. There was, it is true, plenty to curdle the blood in the speeches, which usually consisted of graphic tales of wrongful arrest and shoot-outs with the police. But the ceremonies would invariably con-clude on a note of uplift and sentiment. And the hard cases in shades with gun-holster bulges under their left armpits would respond with vigour to propositions like, 'Can we now have a big hand for black American motherhood?'

On weekends I would spend lazy days in the park with new-found friends, working my way through a stack of joints. On one occasion I lamented the bother of having to roll them, and a friend told me that it was possible to get the active ingredient of marijuana in pill form. Next time we were in the park he produced the pills and the day flew magically by. Years later, when I returned to San Francisco and the same friend, I natu-rally asked him if he could still lay hands on supplies of the active ingredient of marijuana, and he told me not to be such a dumb Limey. We had tripped on LSD.

I never tired of this sybaritic existence, but by the summer of 1968 it was evident that I was not about to find my fortune on the West Coast. I thought perhaps it might be waiting for me in New York. Accordingly I invested fifty dollars of my 'Merch' money in a means of getting there, which proved to be a 1942 Dodge with a sawn-off broom handle holding the fan belt off the engine.

I made the journey across America with a German-American friend from Reed College called Gary Achziger, and his girlfriend, Linda Burnham. A second-generation American, Achziger had turned his back on the family butchery business, and any other business for that matter. Of all the work-shy people I've met he was the most content with total rejection of the puritan work ethic (though I discovered, with some disappointment, that late in life even Achziger compromised by taking on a two-day-a-week job). Since I could not drive and Achziger was often too tired and emotional to drive, this placed a rather heavy burden on Linda. We would ease the problem by giving lifts to hitchhikers. Anyone prepared to drive the decrepit heap for another hundred miles would be given a self-drive lift while Linda slept in the back. With these stratagems we crossed America at the speed of a wagon train, with frequent stops to observe the activities of the indigenous population.

In a populous place called Chicago we came across many men in blue beating up many youngsters in richly varied attire. We learned that the blue men were Mayor Daley's policemen, while the youngsters were demonstrators upset by the defeat of their cause at the Democratic National Convention, where the surviving peace candidate, Eugene McCarthy, had been out-manoeuvred by the old guard. The other peace candidate, called Robert Kennedy, had previously been shot. The young people, very naturally, were in a disillusioned frame of mind. This was a lesson for me. Because my first experience of America had been confined to its more radical West Coast, I had tended to overestimate the forces of liberalism in the society.

Chicago in 1968 was a stern reminder of that other, more reactionary America which was still strong, and still very seriously in business.

We kept heading east until we were rolling up Madison Avenue in New York, where the pavement-bound advertising executives looked at our vehicle with wild surmise. Some of the older ones, probably people who worked on the original Dodge account, broke into spontaneous applause. It was a fairy-tale entry into the city, with a tragic sequel. Next day the Dodge was gone. My first hope was that it had been stolen and that some other insane characters were steering it back across the

continent, picking up hitchhikers. But it appeared that we had parked it illegally, and the police had mistaken it for an abandoned vehicle, and the 1942 Dodge was now enjoying an afterlife as a two by two foot metal cube.

In most other respects New York was good to me. I secured

a commission from *Esquire* magazine in my first week, and I developed a connection with Pushpin Studio, a lively agency run by Seymour Chwast and Milton Glazer, who would soon start up *New York Magazine*, and employ Julian Allen, a good friend of mine from art school, as its first artist reporter.

At night I would retreat to a cockroach-infested hole in the wall on the Lower East Side. At that stage I was trying to save every penny to bring my family over. This made me a rock-hard touch for the unfortunate Bowery bums along my route home, though I would feel compelled to shell out for one who shuffled towards me with the immortal line, 'Have you got fifteen dollars for my ballet lessons?'

Towards the end of the year David King came croaking back into my life. He had been sent over by the *Sunday Times* magazine to assemble illustrative material for its issue on America '68, a year that had been more eventful than most in that it contained two major political assassinations (of Robert Kennedy and Martin Luther King Jr), no end of riots in the cities by disenchanted blacks, turmoil and unrest on every student campus; and a president withdrawing from standing for re-election brought about by anti-war protesters, and it was in the process of being topped off by an electoral choice between Richard Nixon and Hubert Humphrey, which seemed to provide powerful evidence for the survival of the unfittest. King and I discussed which items on this abundant menu he should select for the magazine, but he also took a keen interest in my personal circumstances. He pronounced my living quarters totally unfit for human habitation. Then, out on the street, we saw one hobo leaning over another on the ground, solicitously, we thought at first. Then it became apparent that the leaning hobo was carefully peeling off the fallen hobo's overcoat for his own personal use. King could then see that, by some New York standards, I had it made.

One day he came by with news of a consultation he had just had with Andy Warhol at his Factory. Warhol had apparently urged on him the importance of dealing severely with the commanding heights of the economy. His counsel, as King remembered it, was: 'You've gotta rip off the big organizations, David.' On the strength of this higher wisdom King and I took advantage of his generous *Sunday Times* expense account by going to Max's Kansas City, New York's fashionable artists' bar, where we were able to research the effects of Boilermakers (beer with Bourbon chasers) on the creative temperament.

My main contribution to King's project was my most ambitious model to date, featuring Chicago's Mayor Daley in command of his troops. Daley was modelled in plasticine, but I needed a little more verisimilitude for his men, so I collected two pigs from a slaughterhouse and with a sharp knife adapted them into dancing policemen. I also established that I had not entirely lost touch with events in England by fashioning another model of a desiccated Enoch Powell as a customs officer, poised menacingly over two naked black immigrants in an opened suitcase.

The New Year started brightly enough, but I needed to get my personal documents in apple-pie order before bringing my family over. I had got into a tangle over my visa status but it was nothing serious, so I went to the downtown office of the visa people to straighten things out. I was interviewed there by a woman officer who seemed uncannily well clued up on my movements and contacts, including those with the Panthers and anti-war people in San Francisco. She was, not to put too fine a point on it, unsympathetic to my case. The way she saw it was, 'We have enough trouble-makers like you here without importing any more.' To complicate matters, I was asked to cite a referee, some person who could testify to my sterling personal qualities. I racked my brains to remember the last wholly respectable, bookish, middle-class character I had come across, and it was the father of Linda Burnham, the heroine of the cross-country drive. So I volunteered his name. It was only later that I discovered he was a leading member of the American Communist Party.

Through all this the Pushpin people were very supportive and helped me to get the best legal advice. The legal advice was that I could probably stay in America and successfully fight any deportation order if I was prepared to take on an expensive legal battle that could last for years, and during those years I would almost certainly have to remain separated from my family. But there was another way. If I made the life of the authorities much easier by voluntarily deporting myself, there was no reason why I should not be allowed to return after an interval of two years, with the slate wiped clean. So I thought about the options, and I went quietly.

I came back to England to lick my wounds, and to a new, but thoroughly familiar, home. While I had been in the United States, Deirdre and the children had made a strategic retreat from London to Cambridge, where they were now resident in a tiny house in Orchard Street, near the city centre. It was familiar because my father had bought it ten years earlier for £500. It was part of a terrace scheduled for demolition, but it had provided Deirdre and myself with a marital home in the few months before we bunked off to London. While we were away savouring the delights of metropolitan society the house had suffered from neglect and regular visits by vandals, but it had miraculously escaped demolition. Some alert architect, moved by the rare quality of the mansard roofs, had managed to ensure preservation of the whole terrace. It still stands to this day.

Interestingly enough, all the major emporia in which I actually worked, like the *Observer* building in Tudor Street, the *Sunday Times* headquarters in Gray's Inn Road, and subsequently the first *Spitting Image* factory in Canary Wharf, have all been razed to the ground. There's probably a moral in all this somewhere, but I'd rather not know what it is.

CHAPTER SEVEN

THE COSMIC COUCH

While I had been away in America, Deirdre had fixed up a new home, shored up the family fortunes with some magazine illustration, and capably preserved our two children, somewhat enlarged but still wholly recognizable. I could tell that I had some catching up to do on the bread-winning and parenting fronts. The trouble was I felt so lethargic.

Back at the *Sunday Times* there was a reassuring familiarity. Godfrey Smith still benignly surveyed the troops across his serene desk, Francis Wyndham and Michael Rand still sparked off the big ideas, and David King was still his unmistakable self. My first project for him, which we had discussed earlier in New York, was a model called 'The Assassins', which focused on Lee Harvey Oswald, Sirhan Sirhan and James Earl Ray, the men

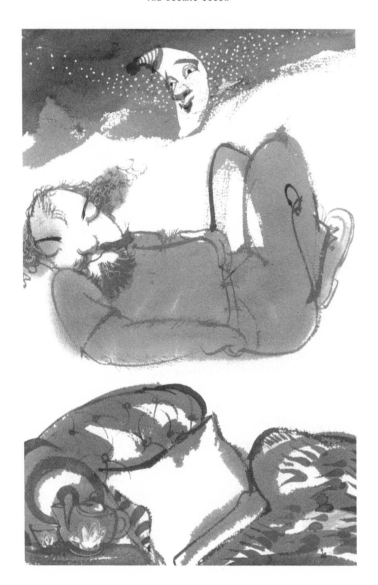

83

who, reportedly at least, had bumped off John Kennedy, Robert Kennedy and Martin Luther King Jr respectively. I did it with a lot of tomato ketchup and with a Stars and Bars background after the style of Jasper Johns, an American artist whom I very much admired. And I was pleased with it, though the work was oddly tiring.

I also had another project on the go about biological engineering, for which I had to construct a reasonably convincing womb and foetus. I made the foetus out of plasticine and the placenta out of a bathroom sponge. I painted them and left them propped up in the art department to dry overnight, and the early-morning cleaners went through the roof. There had been some complaints before about my model-making materials adhering to cherished surfaces, but now it was showdown time. Smith called me in and said there was only one solution to the problem as far as he could see: in future I would have to do the model-making side of my work from home, and this condition would be written into my contract. This punishment was like music to my ears, as I was now very tired indeed.

All the same, I had to go up to London to work on more conventional illustration projects, and there was a very big one in the works. While the men and women of Insight specialized in investigations in depth, the magazine was more noted for what were known as investigations in width, some of which spanned several issues. And Godfrey Smith had come up with the widest one so far conceived, 'The 1,000 Makers of the Twentieth Century'. David King and I were set to work on the design and illustrations. Before we could get to H for Hitler, I keeled over.

The diagnosis was hepatitis. I had it for almost a year, and my memory is of continuously trying to read the same page of a book and continuously giving up. I would lie all day on what

Peter Fluck named 'the Cosmic Couch', the sofa in the front room. Very occasionally I would make heavy-limbed expeditions to the Fitzwilliam Museum to give my eyes something to do. On an approved diet of white meat, nuts and lettuce there was not much pleasure to be had in eating. Drinking was out of the question, and I couldn't even smoke dope as it had the effect of making me itch all over. Not only was I incapable of doing anything, I thought I would never be capable of doing anything again. My loss of confidence was total.

After what seemed an eternity, I began to pick up a little in the summer of 1970 when we spent several weeks in Menorca at a villa presciently acquired by my father. My next-door neighbour there told me that he had made his fortune from the production of brass coffin handles. This inspiration to self-help combined with sun, swimming and consumption of a more edible class of white meat was to some extent restoring, but I was still a long way from being ready to commit myself to any form of work.

Eventually Deirdre kicked me out. She could see that I had shaken off the hepatitis and that I was ultimately suffering from loss of bottle. So it was suitcases on the pavement time, and I was told to go to London and not to bother about coming home until I had managed to put some work together. In London I was received by Peter Fluck, not one of the world's prize-winning male nurses. But he very kindly allowed me to occupy the spare room in his flat, which also served as a studio, off Kensington Church Street.

I could see from the evidence of industry in his studio that our roles had been reversed. Never one to overextend himself, Fluck used to accuse me of running around after too many commissions in order to satisfy a deep psychological need for overwork. Now it appeared to me that Fluck of all people might be prey to a similar condition. While I had been playing Rip Van Winkle he had kept the torch of model-making in Britain shining bright. Under the patronage of Alastair Burnet, the editor of the *Economist*, he had been able to exhibit a series of notorious political specimens on the magazine's front cover. His study of Harold Wilson had been so evil-looking that Michael Heseltine offered to buy it.

Occasionally Alastair Burnet would come by late at night, ricocheting off the walls as he ascended the six flights of stairs to the studio. Checking on work in progress, he would jam his face up close to Fluck's latest grotesque. As an innocent bystander I found it hard to tell which caricature of a face Fluck had been working on. Another of Fluck's regular customers, for both illustrations and grotesques, was the *Radio Times*. Fluck also produced a regular caricature for *Labour Weekly*, the abnormally unsuccessful official party publication. He told me that he liked this work as it allowed him to practise his caricature in print in complete privacy.

Oppressed by all this industry in the home, I fled back to the *Sunday Times*, where David King was ready to put me on the lightest of light duties. And Deirdre was right, it was just my nerve that had gone. Within a few days back at the newspaper I knew I would be equal to anything they could throw at me. Some weeks later, around the beginning of 1971, I was allowed back into the marital home.

Deirdre had always been a moderate person, neither smoking, nor drinking alcohol, nor eating meat. The only thing she liked to excess was me, on occasion. Now, in the wake of my illness and with what seemed like somebody else's metabolism, I too had to learn some of the arts of moderation. This was perhaps overdue in my case, as my consumption of drink and drugs had probably been some way above the national average. My life changed quite radically. I became more regular in my habits and in the time I had once spent enriching the local publicans I now raised rabbits with Sophie and did all manner of wholesome things. However, I did allow myself the occasional relapse.

One of these occurred on the publication of David King's photographic book about Leon Trotsky. We were both drunk and in cheerful state of mind in the West End and I thought it would be a good time to teach my good friend a skill I had not exercised since my student days in Cambridge – how to walk on the roofs of parked cars. Unfortunately one of the cars was a cab, pulling away, which led to my dislocating my ankle. This probably accounted for the leniency with which King and I were treated when we subsequently appeared before Bow Street Magistrates' Court on drunk and disorderly charges.

King was a much more political animal than I could ever be, and he persuaded the *Sunday Times*, which was still Conservative in its editorial outlook, to run a long succession of articles on Lenin, Trotsky and Chairman Mao and other like-minded characters. In the course of this occupation he amassed the finest collection of revolutionary photographs outside the Iron Curtain. He used these extraordinary pictures to make the revolutionary subject-matter more palatable to less radical superior editors. King's other obsession, less controversial politically but not without complications, was with the boxer Cassius Clay, later known as Muhammed Ali.

Not long after my return to work Godfrey Smith was moved to another job, to be replaced by a very young Old Etonian called Magnus Linklater, who from our point of view was very much an unknown quantity. By way of breaking the new editor in to the ethos of the magazine King invited Linklater to come along and watch an Ali versus Joe Frazier fight, being screened live in a Finsbury Park cinema at three o'clock in the morning. It was apparently a scene of the utmost degradation, with an ankle-deep litter of beer cans and broken peanut shells, and a din that could only be made by the best concentration of fighting drunks in London. As they were sitting down, Linklater said in an upper-class *sotto voce* that pierced the atmosphere like a knife: 'What an interesting class of person we have here.' For a few seconds the cinema went deadly quiet, before the din resumed again. To this day King believes he owes his life to the fact that nobody in the upper circle could actually believe the evidence of their own ears.

Linklater, who later edited the *Scotsman*, became a wonderful editor of the magazine. He was as liberal as Smith but much more enthusiastic and, of course, more of our own age. He was a cut above us in the class spectrum, being the son of the novelist Eric Linklater and enjoying high connections in the Scottish aristocracy, but as he went so thoroughly native this never presented any difficulty. The only pity was that he lasted only three years before Harry Evans moved him on to other duties in the more serious parts of the newspaper.

In that time I got to model most of the leading political figures of the day, often as an accompaniment to long feature articles written by Susan Crosland and Hugo Young. There were frustrations, of course. My study of Rupert Murdoch as a macflasher, with a copy of the *Sunday Times* obscuring his erogenous zone, was done at high speed to illustrate an article about the great newspaper proprietor written by Peter Dunn. It then got stuck in the works for eighteen months before Harry

Evans, who had cravenly shown the material to Murdoch, felt he could allow it to appear.

In the course of routine research for a feature on the House of Commons, Tom Driberg had shown King and me around the place and, as an added bonus, detailed the various locations where he had pleasured himself with certain high-ranking persons. We passed all the salient details on to Linklater, whose response was a model of rectitude. The magazine, he said, was no place for a cocksucker's guide to the House of Commons.

This was not quite Driberg's last hurrah, but his health was deteriorating rapidly. He retreated more and more often to his flat in the Barbican, where he endlessly watched television with failing eyes, but with his instincts still wholly intact. I remember visiting him there once when a row of leggy dancing girls flashed up on the screen. Driberg peered and then turned to me and asked, 'Are they really boys?' It seemed an innocent enough lie to say they really were.

I still kept my hand in as a freelance, doing Ken Russell as 'Narcissus' for *Men Only* and Noel Coward for *Nova*, replete with a beautiful set of butterfly wings which Deirdre designed and made from a material called 'Vilene'. In fact most of the models' outfits in this period were made by Deirdre, which accounts for their unusually well turned out appearance.

My great pleasure at this time was going back to the United States on short-term assignments. My own misbehaviour in relation to that country had long since dwindled into insignificance. The only misbehaviour the Americans were seriously interested in now was that of their own government. The spectacle of Richard Nixon, always a caricaturist's dream target on account of his ski-jump nose, being dragged down by the

Watergate scandal was hardly edifying, but it had to be classed as compelling drama. The crisis created a tremendous appetite for Americana in Europe, and I was happy to bring in relief supplies in the form of effigies of bent politicians and bloated capitalists.

On these American journeys I was able to colour in some of the blanks left from my first grand tour. I penetrated the Catskill Mountains, where I met Clarence Schmidt, a quintessential American loony genius, dedicated to the improvement of nature. His specialities were mountain-painting and tree-rearrangements. He would strip down the branches, wrap them in aluminium foil, and then reattach them to the trees to form superior designs. When the light reflected off the lake at the foot of Schmidt's favourite mountain his work acquired a magical quality that could never be replicated in any art gallery. Schmidt told me that in the little time he had to spare he was rewriting the Bible.

I met a more ominous species of nutter in Winnfield, Louisiana, the home town of Huey Long, the South's most notorious political son. 'How long you bin in this country, boy?' the sheriff asked me. Two months, I confessed. 'Goddam,' he said. 'You speak pretty good American.' By day there was almost tangible racial tension about the place, but by ten o'clock in the evening it was asleep, not unlike Littleport in that respect. A local reporter asked me what I thought about the place, obviously wanting me to drop myself in it with some smart-ass liberal remark, but I spoke the simple truth. I said it reminded me of home.

There was one aspect of life on the *Sunday Times*, tolerated by Smith and positively encouraged by Linklater, that very much appealed to me. This could be defined as doing somebody else's thing. I rarely felt trapped in my role as an illustrator or model-maker because, if the inclination took me, I could branch out as a photographer, a story tipster, a picture researcher, a writer's researcher or even a writer.

One of my first assignments in this area involved working with Colin Simpson, an ace Insight investigator with a British Army background. My task was only vaguely defined but it appeared that my main duty would be to act as a back-up witness to his investigations, while taking a few photographs as reference for the colour drawings I was to prepare. Our mission was to look into the affairs of a shady bank in Morocco, and we met by prior arrangement in Gibraltar.

My first surprise in Gibraltar was the discovery of another back-up witness, Simpson's pretty young bride of very recent vintage. So we were honeymooning and investigating at the same time. Stealth was apparently of the essence, so the approach to Morocco was made in a small boat of dubious seaworthiness which Simpson had hired at the quayside. Within twenty minutes of setting foot on Moroccan soil we were all under arrest.

Simpson remonstrated with the cops in his best British gunboat commander style, but they were unmoved. It appeared that coastguards had given them concrete intelligence of the arrival of a smuggler's vessel with a description of the three people on board that fitted us perfectly – one white man, one white woman and one Japanese sumo wrestler. After Simpson had been allowed to make a number of furious phone calls, which must have alerted the rest of North Africa to the arrival of an undercover investigative team, the police started to relent. And when the boat proved to be 'clean' it was convivial mint teas all round.

I had a different kind of education from Murray Sayle, with whom I became more closely acquainted during one of the magazine's investigations in width. This particular one involved saturation coverage of a day in the life of Cambridge, and due to a logistical cock-up we both found ourselves doing the night shift observing Newnham ladies' college for any sign of newsworthy activity. As there was not a lot to report, Sayle gave me the benefits of his wit and wisdom. He was the oldest of the lively tribe of Australians on the *Sunday Times* and he took his responsibilities as an elder seriously. I was more than happy to be his disciple.

Journalism was, he said, essentially about stereotypes, but it was a bad idea to stick with the same ones for too long. He gave Insight, to which he had been a major contributor, as a for instance. Originally it had been based on the twin propositions: 'We name the guilty man. Arrow points to the defective part.' But the genre had been debased by overuse and poor imitation. What was needed now was a new, more warmhearted stereotype. Perhaps 'We name the innocent man,' for a change.

He was inclined to think that travelling in journalism was often more important than actually arriving. This was an understandable prejudice in that Sayle himself was already a great traveller and non-arriver. His first-person articles on *almost* sailing across the Atlantic single-handed and *almost* climbing Everest were among the most popular the newspaper had ever run. On our return to the *Sunday Times* we got down to planning how to *almost* cross the Andes together on folding Moulton bicycles. For weeks thereafter the art department would be disrupted by Sayle's search for the perfect tent for this expedition as he tested out and erected any that seemed capable of the job. Sadly, other work intervened, and our Andes 'Lost World' adventure on wheels never got further than the Blue Lion pub in the Gray's Inn Road.

Though Sayle was one of the best writing journalists on the paper, he never, unlike some lesser writers, implied that there was any great mystique about his activity. The only qualities necessary for a journalist were, he said, 'rat-like cunning, a plausible manner, and a little literary ability'. I knew I could never master a plausible manner but my encounters with Sayle encouraged me to exercise what little literary ability I had, and I eventually assembled a long article about Arno Brecker, Hitler's favourite sculptor, words and pictures, which ran in the magazine.

My scoops included a find of George Grosz's last photomontages in Manhattan, which appeared in the magazine with a selection of previously unpublished letters. I was also a seminal influence on the inquiry into supermarket codes, which effectively concealed the antiquity of the food people bought in the shops. This latter achievement led to debates in the House of Commons, a change in the law and crusading appearances on television by Harry Evans. And all because I'd clipped the original story out of the *San Francisco Bay Guardian* and imported the cutting to inspire a British version.

My scoop that got away was a marvellous collection of *fin de siècle* drawings and erotica by Miklos Vadash, who had been one of the leading illustrators on *L'Assiette au Beurre*. They belonged to an elderly relative of Vadash who lived in St John's Wood and whom I would occasionally visit. I once took Paul Hogarth along and he thought the material was 'almost as good as Lautrec'. I had hoped to get some of it for the magazine but the old man could never bring himself to release it. After his death I heard that a lot of the stuff had found its way into the collection of Victor Lowndes, the *Playboy* supremo.

My most unlikely assignment for the magazine was covering an officers' training course at Sandhurst with Jeffrey Bernard, whose column in the *Spectator* became known as 'the longest suicide note in history'. I thought I was in luck as Bernard was on the wagon at the time, but his laid-back style remained unimpaired by sobriety. So I found myself clambering over obstacle courses and pounding the parade ground while he sweated it out in the officers' mess eating toast and honey and talking cricket.

Despite his wholly deserved reputation as a boozer, I never saw Bernard actually buy a drink for someone else, at least not until years later when I happened to bump into him in the Coach and Horses in Soho. He had just seen, and approved of, one of my shows on TV. I know this because he furtively pressed a fiver into my palm, with the words, 'Enjoyed the show, take this and don't tell anyone I bought you a drink.' Now, I think, this lapse can be revealed.

The most exciting assignment for me was covering the Portuguese revolution and the fall of Salazar. I did this in conjunction with Alex Mitchell, another spirited Australian, who provided me with a list of contacts and wrote up the dispatches I sent back from Lisbon. I went around collecting secret police files which had been scattered in the streets and generally hoovering up an incredible atmosphere. At one point I saw a mass of fired-up sailors and soldiers issuing from a cinema. I looked up at the hoarding to see what was so exciting, and they were showing Eisenstein's *Battleship Potemkin*. My main task was picking up pictures and statements from people who had been tortured by the Salazar regime. These were not in short supply.

There were some hard-left journalists on the *Sunday Times*, though many fewer than Rupert Murdoch liked to imagine. But for the most part they were talkers, rather than doers. Alex Mitchell was an exception. Though a very entertaining writer he took a major salary cut to work on *Ink*, a short-lived revolutionary publication, and an even bigger one to become Editor of *Newsline*, the official newspaper of Gerry Healy's Trotskyite Workers' Revolutionary Party which, like most such parties, ended in acrimony and tears.

Many of Mitchell's old mates on the *Sunday Times* would go on about the waste of his talent, but I never looked at it in that light. I could not bring myself to join any political party, partly on the Groucho Marxist principle that I should not belong to any organization that was foolish enough to have me, but mainly because I knew I was congenitally incapable of toeing a party line. But I was also very grateful for the existence of parties of the far left, and I would readily supply *Ink* and *Newsline* and other similar organs with low-cost cartoons and caricatures. It seemed to me then, and to some extent now, that they were the only agencies through which working-class people could get an education in what capitalism was all about. Unfortunately, they have no talent whatsoever for telling people what Communism was all about.

CHAPTER EIGHT

LUCK AND FLAW

People who once worked for the *Sunday Times* almost invariably have their own personal idea of when the rot set in, and things changed inexorably for the worse. A popular date for whingers of this type is 1983, when the rough-hewn Andrew Neill arrived as editor and vigorously set about dispersing the last lost tribes of Harry Evans. More popular still is 1981, when Rupert Murdoch took over as proprietor and began to stamp his unique imprint on the organization. Some others make a sound case for 1978, when the combined stupidity of the pre-Murdoch management and the print unions succeeded in keeping the paper off the streets for a whole year. I personally, however, would date my own whinge even earlier, to late 1974 when the advertising and marketing departments first seriously got their grappling hooks into the magazine.

By that time the *Sunday Times* had long since lost its novelty value and was in fierce competition with the *Observer* and *Telegraph*, and later many others, for colour advertising revenue. The way ahead, the advertising people thought, was to make the magazine much more consumer-orientated, essentially making the editorial content serve their perceptions of the needs of the market. Magnus Linklater, to his credit, thought this was a lousy idea, and said so. Within a few months he was summarily relieved of his command, and replaced by Hunter Davies who took to the journalism of how to mow your lawn, how to buy your car and how to brush your dog's teeth, like a duck to water.

Davies was a capable writer and a clever man, but his horizon tended to be somewhat limited. He was fond of saying that anything worth doing could be done between the hours of nine and five, which could conceivably be true for a Cumbrian bank clerk but did not seem to accord with the experience of any truly creative people I had come across. Matters beyond Dover were of modest interest, and even ideas on the home front tended to be treated warily unless they were sanctified by being in the current news, or signposted by PR blurbs. The old magazine's emphasis on trying to break original stories on the 'You saw it here first' principle went into decline.

The advertisers had always been inclined to kick up when their products appeared in issues featuring Don McCullin's searing war pictures. For a while they had nothing to worry about as Davies had the world's greatest war photographer taking snaps of Hadrian's Wall and Consett in County Durham. McCullin's talent was so great that his work would eventually reassert itself and find a place, but my skills and those of David

King were beyond accommodation. King was accustomed to a tremendous flexibility when laying out each issue, but the adverts were now placed throughout the magazine in a way that broke up most of the best spreads. This was no impediment to the little word-bite consumer-orientated stories that were the order of the day, but it was the enemy of any grand design. It goes without saying that caricature models of famous and distinguished people were not a prized item. Michael Rand, our main supporter in the magazine's commanding heights, was shifted to the newspaper shortly after Linklater's departure and replaced by Edwin Taylor, a designer more attuned to the requirements of the new regime. As he went, Rand said to King and myself, 'Boys, the party's over.' But he didn't have to tell us.

In the doldrums that ensued I remember being summoned into the Editor's office, where Harry Evans seemed to have something on his mind. He asked me what I was doing exactly. So I told him about some of the more interesting things, like making model caricatures for the *New York Times* and *Der Spiegel*, and about the plans I had to bring out an illustrated version of Charles Dickens's *A Christmas Carol* for Penguin Books. I was just about to tell him about a new line in ceramic mugs I was exploring when I saw that the great Editor's eyes were glazing over. 'No,' said Evans, 'I meant, what are you doing for us?' The answer was not a lot. Whereas once I had done about 80 per cent of my work for the *Sunday Times* with the other 20 per cent freelance, these proportions had been effectively reversed.

There was never any major row. I simply stopped volunteering ideas, and very few were offered to me. My contributions to the magazine, like those of David King and Francis Wyndham, simply withered away. And eventually I was let go.

Though it was on offer, I did not take any redundancy money because I reckoned I must have got that before I left. Years later I bumped into Davies at a magazine reunion bash where he remarked that I'd done so well in television that perhaps I should thank him for firing me from the magazine. I might have done, if he had acted so decisively. But the truth was that he simply bored me slowly out of the building.

I invested some of my unearned income from the *Sunday Times* in a place of worship. This was a small temperance chapel in earlier times, though latterly an abandoned monument to dry rot. It was located only a few hundred yards from our home in Orchard Street, and I bought it for £1,500. Deirdre, like the *Sunday Times* before her, had expressed enthusiasm to locate my model-making at some other address, and the chapel was it.

As my freelance activity expanded, principally through contacts in the United States, I invited Deirdre to share the workload in a full business partnership. She responded to this glittering opportunity by saying it was probably the worst idea I had had in my entire life. I was therefore obliged to be inordinately nice to Peter Fluck.

We already had a name for a partnership, Luck and Flaw. It had been bestowed on us back in our college days by Alec Heath, the head of the art school, as he was changing his trousers. Our tutors were always changing their trousers in those days before rushing off to be seen at some smart university event. On one such occasion a young member of staff had burst in on Heath, trousers round ankles; he looked up and said, 'For God's sake close the door before that awful pair Luck and Flaw see me like this.'

The first big job we did together was a series of models

featuring the candidates running in the 1976 presidential election. This was interesting because when the *New York Times* first commissioned me to do the work they insisted on my going down to Washington and making the acquaintance of my political victims. I had never been all that keen on meeting the people I caricatured in case they exhibited some redeeming qualities which could spoil my aim. But as it was part of the commission I did as requested, and I was escorted round the offices of a variety of Senators by Ruth Ancel, the newspaper's art director, and introduced as 'the illustrator' for the paper's election coverage. It did not spoil my aim to any marked degree. In the case of Hubert Humphrey, the archetype of the flesh-pressing, glad-handing political operator, I was unable to spot any redeeming features. I did not take to Edward Kennedy very much either, despite our common feature – the tell-tale red rings round the end of the nose that denote a long-time fondness for booze. But Kennedy was at least smart. Of all the politicians I saw, he was the only one curious enough to ask what my 'illustrations' consisted of. 'Ah,' he grunted, when I explained, 'so you're the hangman.'

There was, however, one aspect of this itinerary that I did find slightly disturbing. The politician I found far and away the most likeable was Barry Goldwater, the standard-bearer of the extreme right. It occurred to me that if, by some horrible mischance, I was obliged to go into the jungle I'd rather have Goldwater as a companion than any of the Kennedy clan.

The *New York Times* was good, high-profile stuff for the partnership, but there were limits to what we could do. Fluck and I had the idea of doing George Wallace, the crippled Segregationist candidate, emerging from his wheelchair and racing away on his hands, over the caption, 'Up and running.'

This was deemed some way beyond the limits. No such constraint was necessary when we worked for *National Lampoon*, the Washington-based satirical magazine, where our contact editor was Tony Hendra, who had once strutted the boards in the Cambridge Footlights with John Cleese.

At our first meeting Hendra asked me if I would consider doing a model of Mel Brooks in chopped chicken liver. I knew then that we were on the same wavelength. Hendra gave us a king-sized order for a series of ten satirical caricatures, each representing a different country in what was to be called the United States of Europe. They were all published in great style, with the exception of Italy. This was in no way untypical of the whole output, featuring as it did an Italian Euro-soldier behaving in a cowardly and sexually rampant manner, so why not Italy? 'Do you want two pairs of broken legs?' asked Hendra, 'Who do you think distributes this goddam paper?'

Fluck and I settled down in the chapel, producing models at a steady clip of forty a year, about three of which we thought were reasonably good. Like all couples forced into extreme intimacy, we became odd, with our own individual curmudgeonly ways. Fluck would disguise his envy of my ability as a salesman of grotesque ideas by saying that I only got orders by threatening to kill people, which was largely untrue. I would mask my resentment of Fluck's superior ingenuity by saying that the only reason he thought laterally was because he was too lazy to think like any normal human being, which was largely true.

When some crucial deadline approached, I used to watch Fluck out of the corner of my eye with appalled fascination. He would drop some vital tool off the bench, but instead of stooping and picking it up like any sane person, he would set to work making a replacement tool from the odds and sods on the bench. If I dared to say anything, he would fudge the issue with a crafty remark like, 'It's too hot to bend down.' As a matter of fact, during the summer months it was too hot in all positions. We had no end of experts coming to counsel us on how to improve the ventilation in the chapel, but the best advice, admittedly given by a very highly qualified architect, was that we should wear kaftans.

I never doubted my partner's ability, but I did sometimes have paranoid worries about his ability to exercise his ability. These worries came over me once when I was in Addenbrooke's Hospital with a suspected kidney complaint. As it happened, my brother Martin, who has a similar physical configuration to my own, was visiting me at the time. He very generously consented to occupy my bed while I went round to the chapel to check up on Fluck's activity quotient. I need not have worried. Fluck was working away as good as gold. But it proved to be an alarming day for Martin. When I crept back to the hospital I found that he had been given my routine test for blood pressure, and it had proved higher than the previous level recorded by his sick brother.

The yin and yang of the Luck and Flaw partnership consisted essentially of me thinking up undoable ideas, and Fluck figuring out ways of doing them, if only to spite me. His most superlative achievement was working out how to make twenty-six caricatures dance for Mr Fezziwig's Ball in our version of *A Christmas Carol*, though his creation of a vomit-gun to demonstrate the effects of English cuisine on a fastidious palate was a very close runner-up. Fluck was also responsible for the credible modelling of life-size hands, which led directly to one of the great leaps forward in our work.

In the early days all our models were relatively small, with big heads and little bodies. Inevitably, each model would have to have its own little made-to-measure outfit. Although Fluck took over from Deirdre as dresser to the models, it was evident, even to me, that the task was a bit on the thankless side. The reason for this was that the real end product of our work was not so much the model itself but the photograph of it, the transparency which would be used by the magazines and newspapers. Once we had photographed a caricature we scrunched it up and used the plasticine to make another one. Its exquisitely crafted little togs would just be thrown away or used to muck out the kitchen sink. I knew that Deirdre found the disposable aspect of the work highly repellent, and Fluck was none too keen on it either.

The answer, of course, was to go life-size with the models, which would give them the choice of a vast range of classy gear from jumble sales and Oxfam. Going life-size would also spare us the problem of miniaturizing all the props. Instead of wielding little wooden axes, they could wield real axes. But we resisted going life-size for a long time, mainly because we could never make hands that did not look like a bunch of bananas. But Fluck cracked it in the end, and vastly extended our range.

My relief from these adventures in the chapel would be to go to London once a week and teach at Hornsey College of Art. It is probably true to say that many of the students were more into music – mainly of the punk variety – than they were into art, but they were a lively bunch, if not a breath of fresh air. One year I sat on the selection committee for incoming students. Naturally I was looking out for kids with talent, and I found one lad who was quite amazing. I wanted him in but I was firmly told that this was not possible even if his work rivalled Rembrandt's. The boy had no O or A Levels and therefore could not qualify for a degree. And if the college could not muster its quota of degrees it would receive less funding. It was interesting to realize that I was teaching on a course to which I could no longer gain admittance as a student, but the whole thing seemed like a crying shame.

I liked teaching because there is nearly always something you can pass on, perhaps not so much a skill but something more like a set of connections. All illustration has its family tree, and if you know about the tree you can introduce young people to branches of it that might engage their interest or, better still, enthusiasm. Paul Hogarth did something like that for Fluck and myself, and I felt it was something I could do for others. I think I managed it to some extent at Hornsey, but perhaps not quite so well at the Central School, to which I ill-advisedly transferred. The fault was not in the students, but in some of the staff, who seemed to me to be absurdly pretentious.

One day I took all the newspapers, from the *Sun* to the *Guardian*, in to the Central and doled them out to my class with the request that each design a front page with as its main banner headline, 'The Queen is Dead'. Anyone who had seen a newsroom going into convulsions at the rumour of the Queen going anywhere near a hospital would realize I was paying these students the compliment of setting them one of the toughest tasks in journalism. And anyone who had not seen such a thing should at least be able to perceive that the task was demanding. But I was hauled before the department head and reprimanded for setting the students 'a frivolous exercise'.

The real frivolity, unhappily, was much of the formal teaching, which was of the how-to-design-a-rain-map-for-Swaziland variety, esoteric and off-putting. The head of department told me that the only reason he had hired me was because the college had stipulated that he must have an illustrator on his team. Personally, he could do without one, especially one whose work was so utterly self-indulgent. My counter-argument was that teaching students how to get paid for expressing their real selves might in the long run, even at the risk of self-indulgence, prove to be more advantageous to them than crabbed exercises in producing useful diagrams of how to load your camera, and suchlike – and in the short run it was certainly a lot less boring. He was not convinced. I taught there against the prevailing ethos for a while until the moment when I had to leave came to me with extreme clarity. A young student there showed me four sheets of artwork in colour, all based on household objects. The presentation was quite stunning, and I heard myself saying, 'These are absolutely beautiful. You really should go to art school.'

Within the Luck and Flaw partnership there was a powerful amount of education in progress. One caricature we did for *National Lampoon* featured Euro-cop, based on the simple concept of a policeman laying into a demonstrator with his truncheon. We did it with a lot of ketchup and it was very, very gory. We also did a sanitized version that turned out to be visually much more horrific than the gory one. This, we realized, was because in the cleaned-up version the person looking at the image felt as if they were participating in a brutal act that was just about to happen. The ostensibly more gruesome picture, on the other hand, was something that had already happened in which the viewer had no participation and therefore no emotional involvement.

A more predictable discovery was the difficulty of caricaturing people or characters you positively liked. I doubt whether P.G. Wodehouse could have a greater admirer than me. On my trips to America I would always read him at 30,000 feet to ensure, if anything went wrong, that I would go down laughing. So we were delighted when an American publisher asked us to model Bertie, Jeeves and Aunt Agatha, but we never got them remotely right.

When in doubt about how to tackle a subject we tended to steal from our favourite old masters, William Hogarth and James Gillray. Fortunately there is no such thing as intellectual property in caricature ideas and, perhaps less fortunately, human nature doesn't change. So lifting the concepts of our long-deceased betters never presented a problem to us, or, I might add, to most other working caricaturists. The first time Fluck and I stole from Gillray was when we were short of an idea for how to illustrate a feature article about Colonel Tom Parker's Svengali-like hold over a rapidly thickening Elvis Presley. We filched Gillray's *Fashion Before Ease,* a cautionary comment on the dangers of the French Revolution depicting the revolutionary corset-maker Tom Paine trying to lace Britannia into a French corset. Admittedly our effort was less geopolitical, but it was just as direct. We had Colonel Parker tightening the corset of an obese Elvis before propelling him on stage.

As the only member of the partnership with a driving licence Fluck was automatically the transport officer, responsible for driving the models down to London where they could be photographed at their best in the studio of our heroic young photographer, John Lawrence Jones. Loading the Citroen Dyane with models was always a major event. To prevent them smashing each other to pieces on the journey we used to have to cement them to the steel floor of the vehicle with lumps of hot plasticine. I used to brew up the old plasticine and hurl great gobs of it down from the upper level of the chapel onto Fluck as he stood by the car below. And Fluck would leap up and down with rage, not having my keen sense of humour.

The humour of John Lawrence Jones also proved a little shaky when we punched holes in his sets, and generally wrecked his studio in pursuit of the right lighting formulae for *A Christmas Carol*, but he came through it all more heroic than ever. Fluck and I always considered that a good photograph could add 40 per cent to the quality of the models, which was why we considered it worth taking them to a specialist studio in London rather than getting a photographer to come to the chapel to take snaps. If our models were in any way more vivid than those of Daumier and other model-makers in the past, it was almost entirely due to developments in colour photography. We were lucky in the technology of our age, much as Aubrey Beardsley, whose black ink style coincided so perfectly with the development of the line block, was lucky in his. Arguably Charles Keene was Beardsley's superior as a draughtsman, but we only got to see his work in the cruder form of wood engravings.

I read somewhere that Rodin shared our enthusiasm for high-grade photography of his product, though for a slightly different reason. As his sculptures lacked portability, he would use photography to whet the interest of prospective clients around the world. We may not have been in the same league as Rodin, but we knew how to stick with the best in this department. My son Shem now art directs the *Radio Times* and if he has a particularly difficult shoot he 'phones Lawrence Jones'. John has been the family photographer for thirty-five years.

By the end of the seventies Luck and Flaw was a truly international business. Our study of Jimmy Carter had gone right round the world and even Venezuela had coughed up its £30 royalty fee. Our presentation of the Queen and Prince Philip feasting on a corgi appeared not only in *Stern* magazine, which had commissioned the work, but also on the cover of the Australian edition of *Time* magazine. In Britain we still serviced the *Economist* and the *Radio Times* and occasionally the *Sunday Times*, where we had become a mild flavour again, not I think because we were much admired, but because they did not want to be left out. The *Sunday Times* business, in any event, tended to be on the cautious side, especially after Rupert Murdoch became its proprietor. I do not think the new owner's satiric instinct extended much beyond appointment of new editors – Andrew Neill for the *Sunday Times* and Kelvin MacKenzie for the *Sun*. We did an excellent study of the comedian Bernard Manning throttling a microphone in the shape of a Pakistani for the *Sunday Times*, but it never appeared. If we wanted to do anything racy, like the Tory Cabinet full frontal in the nude, we would have to turn to outlets like *Men Only*.

Along with the international reputation, we were enjoying a little of the notoriety that our personalities so pathetically craved. Anglia Television and the BBC's *Arena* both did programmes about us. Anthony Wall, the producer of the *Arena* programmes who became a friend, billed us handsomely as the most famous unknown illustrators in Britain.

We were also going broke. The problem with the global business was that, while it was wide, it was quite exceptionally thin. All the overseas stuff was done on perilously fragile margins, and the British market was not that hot either. For filling a space in a magazine or newspaper, which was our essential end-product, we might be paid a little over the rate for the page, but not much. A cartoonist or a photographer working on their own might easily fill the same space with a day's work, whereas no matter how hard I lashed Fluck, or how much he needled me, the two of us could never produced a decent model, properly attired and photographed, in much less than a week.

It was a hard thing to admit that cornering the international market in grotesques was about as economically rewarding as being a gardener in an Oxbridge college. On the other hand, I do not think that either of us regretted the decision to go it alone together, so to speak, on our home turf. Fluck's idea of heaven was to kit himself out in waders and give any trout in the vicinity a miserable time. This bizarre activity was far more accessible in Cambridge than it had ever been in Kensington. For my part, I very much appreciated the advantages of working so close to home that I could watch Shem, Sophie and Sophie's rabbits growing up. Unlike the children, the rabbits were showing encouraging signs of not wanting to go to art school.

Freed from chores on the models, Deirdre was able to pursue her interest in patchwork and quilting, where her use of complex 'Colourwash' techniques earned her an international reputation as both designer and teacher. Among the overseas places that sought her advice was Soweto in South Africa, and she visited the township on a couple of occasions. I can remember a return match when the ladies of Soweto came to visit us in Orchard Street. It was well known that Soweto was the worst slum in Africa. Less well known was the fact that it also contained an awesome, house-proud bourgeoisie, and I could tell from the horrified expressions of the contingent of black ladies in our dishevelled living room that our housekeeping was well below the standards to which they were accustomed.

Despite the highly connubial nature of our existences, there was no concealing the fact that the most important woman in the lives of Fluck and myself was becoming Mrs Margaret Thatcher. Very soon after her election in 1979 I remember telling Hugo Young, then the deeply sagacious political correspondent of the *Sunday Times*, what a laugh her manifesto was, full of ridiculous pledges that would never be kept. Young felt he should advise me not to get too carried away with mirth, because she was not joking. We did her for the *Sunday Times* as an Iron Maiden, festooned with heavy metal kitchen utensils.

Less successfully, Fluck and I tried to do her as a hen for the *Arena* programme. Through my agricultural connections we found a brilliant hen, which could do practically anything. We kitted her out with a Mrs Thatcher mask and rehearsed her carefully to defecate over some 'Top Secret' Cabinet papers on a desk. But when the cameras were rolling she only seemed to be interested in undoing the cameraman's shoelaces. In the end I just took her home with me, where she defecated over everything but paid her way by laying an egg for my breakfast every morning.

When making caricatures, or indeed anything else, it is possible to get too close to your own work. We might think something was funny, but this was not always the best guide to how a caricature would be viewed by the outside world. Whenever we finished one we would call in our Sudanese milkman for his expert opinion. He took the task most seriously, and saved us on several occasions. It was the milkman too who urged us to hurry along to the Fitzwilliam Museum where the ceramic grotesques by the Martin Brothers, Britain's first serious art potters, were being exhibited. We were impressed and a new department of the business, Luck and Flaw's 'Ugly Mugs', was established almost on the spot.

We made, for popular use, several thousand Mrs Thatcher

teapots which, aside from certain deficiencies, such as a tendency to dislocate the wrist of anyone over 30 and to scald hands of all ages, were really very fine objects. Unfortunately, outside Northern Ireland, where they appeared to think they were a Tory Central Office promotion, they did not sell in significant numbers. We therefore had plenty to spare when Anglia TV came round to make their little programme about our work. The final question they asked on camera was, 'And why should anyone buy a Mrs Thatcher teapot?' With uncanny foresight we had managed to anticipate this question and had set up three Mrs Thatcher teapots on a glass table. As the camera panned over them I moved in with a large hammer and smashed the lot. At this point the commentator's voice, unscripted by us, said, 'What a wonderful way to earn a living.'

Somehow we attracted the attention of a character called Robert Putz, who was an exceptionally enjoyable German businessman. He came into the chapel one day and immediately ingratiated himself by announcing, 'Chennelmen, I am going to make you both millionaires.' Putz even had us making, theoretically for Nikon Cameras, a rainbow with a puzzled chameleon standing in front of it. One day we were humping this enormous chameleon around when it hit us both simultaneously that never in 8 million years was this idea going to work. So the chorus went up, 'What a wonderful way to earn a living.'

The truth of the matter was that we found it difficult to take the advertising world seriously, though we did try to some extent. I remember one time we spent over an hour kicking our heels in the waiting room of some advertising mogul in the West End. The main feature of this room was that it was festooned with glass cases containing 'Golden Arrows', one of the highest accolades in the advertising business. When the award-winning man deigned to come out and see us, Fluck said, 'I never knew you were so remarkably fond of archery.'

I must say I did admire Fluck's preference for losing a commission to a jest, but even I sometimes wished he could bring himself to rein in his satirical instinct. The only other partnership we knew of that played with plasticine for a living were the Aardmans in Bristol. Peter Lord and David Sproxton made stop-motion films and would later become justifiably famous and showered with Oscars for *Creature Comforts*, *Wallace and Gromit* and *Chicken Run*. When I first met them I was deeply impressed by their solidarity. On all matters relating to their work and its presentation it was impossible to put a razor blade between them. This was never the way of Luck and Flaw, which seemed to derive much of its energy from mutual derogation if only, as they say, in fun. And as we did not take each other seriously, we could hardly complain when others took a leaf out of the same book.

Before publication of our *A Christmas Carol*, on which we had lavished enormous effort, the BBC sent Sally Hardcastle from the *Today* programme to interview us about the book. Fluck insisted on taking the lead and inventively, but not strictly relevantly, answering all her questions with the titles of Charles Dickens's books. Thus:

Hardcastle: 'Were the illustrations difficult to do?'
Fluck: 'We had *Hard Times*.'
Hardcastle: 'How do you like working for Penguin Books?'
Fluck: 'A *Bleak* publishing *House*.'
Hardcastle: 'Will children like such grotesque illustrations?'
Fluck: 'We have *Great Expectations*.'

And so on, until an exasperated Hardcastle flicked off her tape-recorder and swept huffily out of the chapel. Another golden opportunity to promote our wares bit the dust. On publication another journalist asked 'Don't you think bringing out an illustrated *Christmas Carol* for the Christmas market a little meretricious of you?' to which Fluck replied 'And a meretriciousmas to you too.'

I have another *Christmas Carol* story which nobody believes but which I'm obliged to relate on account of its being true. In the quest for an American publisher for the book I flew to New York, where indifference reigned. I couldn't find a single publisher even ready to discuss the book, let alone buy it. Looking around the bookshops I happened to notice that many of the prime best-sellers were books about how to cook

113

chicken. I then re-rang a select hit-list of publishers to say that I had a book for sale called *Chicken Dishes of the World*, which had lavish illustrations. This led to almost instant appointments with a range of top commissioning editors.

Oddly enough, none of them expressed any great surprise on finding that I was selling Dickens not chickens. In London I would probably have been promptly shown the door, but in New York there seems to be a presumption that anyone inventive enough to trick their way in might, conceivably, also have something worthwhile to offer. In fact the man at Simon & Schuster was almost too enamoured with what I had to offer. His thought was that we could all do big business simply by expanding the concept to illustrating the complete works of Charles Dickens – a project that would have taken Fluck and me several lifetimes to complete. In the end I did a more modest deal at St Martin's Press with a realist who said, 'Well, it ain't Walt Disney, but I'll print a few and see what happens.'

It was nice to have *A Christmas Carol* launched on both sides of the Atlantic, but our *Treasure Island*, which we felt was technically superior in many respects, was still stalled, endlessly waiting for an original publisher ready to take on the expense of its production. Meantime, it was becoming clear that our vigorous efforts to sell out on the advertising and merchandising fronts were both going no place fast. An accountant we called in to advise us on ceramic sales told us that we would be in a more profitable line of business if we went out on the street and bought pound notes for £1.50 a time.

More worryingly, it was becoming apparent that the general feature magazines, always our staple outlet, were all headed down the dread consumerist road that led to *Lifestyles* and *Living Kitchens* and the most short-sighted human horizons.

Luck and Flaw enterprises was, in short, on the verge of discovering a wonderful way not to earn a living when a man announcing himself as Martin Lambie-Nairn came on the telephone and invited us out to lunch.

Lambie-Nairn turned out to be a nice, gnome-like man who did the graphics for current affairs shows at London Weekend Television, and of the many nice things about him the nicest from the point of view of Fluck and myself was that he had some money. The idea in itself was not that novel. Fluck and I had been talking and fantasizing about making the models move almost since the partnership began. One of the main parties to these hitherto fruitless discussions was Pat Gavin, once a student of mine at Hornsey Art School, who had risen, via experience in animation films, to the dizzying height of head of graphics at LWT. It was Gavin who pointed Lambie-Nairn in our direction, and it was Gavin who alerted us to the need to refrain from eating peas off our knives during the lunch.

We were rewarded with Lambie-Nairn's proposal, which was that his own graphics firm, which was doing quite well, should invest some of its surplus cash in a Muppet-style political television programme. It looked as if the cash could be enough to fund our efforts for as long as six months. Would we be interested? Despite my lingering aversion to puppets, we had no hesitation in saying that we would be delighted to spend his firm's money. It would be another two years, by which time we would spend several other people's money, including what was left of our own, before we had anything worthwhile to show for this initiative.

CHAPTER NINE

HERE'S ONE i MADE EARLiER

There were many possible wrong turnings on the road to *Spitting Image*, and Peter Fluck and I managed to take most of them. What sustained us was the dream of bringing our caricature creations to life. What surprised us was the degree to which our own lives were changed by realizing this seemingly innocent fantasy.

There are three basic approaches to animation, and we looked at them all over the years. The classic approach, made famous by Walt Disney, is cell animation, in which movement in the characters is produced by hundreds upon hundreds of drawings, tracing their activity frame by frame, not unlike a flick book. But what was good enough for *Sleeping Beauty* and *Pinocchio* and for Chuck Jones's *Bugs Bunny* did not seem immediate enough for us. And there was another significant consideration. In the days before advances in computer technology offered huge economies by rendering much of the hand work obsolete, full cell animation could come in at anything up to £1,000 a second. On the basis of our original budget, this would have us into overspend in next to no time.

A more accessible form of animation is stop motion, most brilliantly deployed in recent times in the *Wallace and Gromit* films, fashioned by the Oscar-winning Nick Park of Aardman in Bristol. In this type of animation you start out with three-dimensional figures, not vastly different from the ones we were already making, and then move them by very slow degrees, clicking away at each halt to build up the animation, again frame by frame – 25 frames a second. We were initially very attracted to stop motion, but the constraint we kept coming up against was time. It had always been our notion that the models should move in a topical environment. There was no way that stop motion could be fast enough.

We then came, almost by default, to the third main form of animation, namely puppetry. The advantage of puppets is that they can be filmed in real time, but, from my own experience of filming them at Reed College, I could not be persuaded that string puppets were a realistic way ahead. There were, however, in Jim Henson's *Muppets*, graphic examples of what could be achieved by puppeteers using direct hands-up-the-throat techniques.

Despite the huge success of the *Muppets* we were by no means convinced that this approach was entirely right for us. I remember going to a lecture by Henson in which he explained that the Muppets were successful precisely because they were not people. With Kermit, a piece of green rag with two ping-pong balls for eyes, there were no problems of credibility – he was a veritable frog. Kermit could get away with it, even to the extent of telling a TV interviewer that the secret of his success was 'Not blinking'. Henson thought it unlikely that anyone could achieve anything like the same suspension of disbelief with caricatured puppet people.

We thought it might be possible, but only with the most sophisticated puppetry, and that, we reasoned, meant getting seriously acquainted with the film industry. It was clear from films like *Star Wars* and *Greystoke* that the movies were light years ahead of the other media in terms of special effects. Our original idea was that we should design the puppets while film people, with their advanced notions of radio-control and how to make noses explode, et cetera, would kit them out. This was a wrong turning almost from the very start, which set us back at least eighteen months.

By the autumn of 1982 our star caricature, Nancy the parrot, designed to perch on President Reagan's pirate shoulder, had enough metal in her head to fly to the moon. Mechanized controls governed the head, neck and eyelid movements, while the beak, tongue and wings were hand-operated. She was coming in at around £6,000, and for our purposes she was worse than useless. With any luck she would blink on command on one occasion out of five.

What we had totally failed to grasp was the fact that film puppets are essentially one-performance creatures. If they could blink or pick their noses once in a close-up, it was quite enough. But we needed puppets that could credibly go the distance, or at least the length of a pilot programme. The effect of Nancy the Parrot on the morale of our backers, who now included the Cambridge inventor-businessman Clive Sinclair, was not good. They would send emissaries round to the chapel to check on progress, and Fluck, now emerging as the diplomat in the partnership, would assure them that we were making great strides in learning what not to do.

What we had to do was start again. This we did, though not soon enough to retain Sinclair's sponsorship, and he pulled out after investing £20,000 in the venture. Fortunately John Banks, the Cambridge business consultant who was our contact with Sinclair, was subsequently able to recruit another backer to limit the damage. But the main skill I developed during this period was a 'Trust me', Arthur Daley telephone manner when assuring suppliers their cheques were in the post.

Things only really started to look up when we smashed Nancy, and Fluck distributed her bits and pieces among three other puppets. As it turned out, we were quite capable of making small conventional latex puppets ourselves. Eye movements were a problem, but Fluck was confident he could crack it. The biggest problem for both of us was trying to eradicate some of the habits we had spent twenty years learning in newspapers and magazines.

With a newspaper caricature we would invariably start off with the idea, or the joke, before we even thought of reaching for the plasticine, because this would determine whether we wanted our character to be full face or profile and what his or her expression should be. When it came to puppet-creation, however, the one-joke approach was of no value. We had to go against our natural grain and find more neutral expressions that would make our characters capable of telling a lot of jokes, most of them not of our devising.

In late 1982 as our puppet efforts began to show more promise we were joined by some serious jokers in a company called

Spitting Image. The first to join us was Tony Hendra, our old mate from the *National Lampoon,* whom we judged to be the funniest. Hendra was the man who invented the 'Not' concept, producing publications like *Not the Bible* and *Not the New York Times.* The second to arrive was John Lloyd, a young but experienced broadcaster who had borrowed the 'Not' concept to produce *Not the Nine O'Clock News,* a successful BBC comedy programme starring Rowan Atkinson, Mel Smith and Griff Rhys Jones. The third was Jon Blair, a South African documentary producer who would later provide the inspiration for the *Spitting Image* song, 'I've Never Met a Nice South African'. Blair may have been no great shakes as a joker, but he was incredibly effective on the business front. It was Blair who hawked our flimsy wares around the television network and ultimately managed to link us up with Central Television, which agreed to underwrite our further endeavours. In consequence the last lap of the research process – making a pilot programme – was done in some style.

Produced by John Lloyd, scripted by Richard Curtis and Ben Elton, and directed by Phillip Casson, a former *Muppets* director, the *Spitting Image* pilot programme was shot at Ewart Studios in Wandsworth in June 1983, and it turned out rather well. The pilot was never shown publicly, nor is it ever likely to be. The original reason for this was contractual. Performance fees, which we were asked to keep to a minimum, were much lower for a pilot than a transmitted programme. Now of course it is well out of date, though some of its vignettes still have resonance – an Israeli premier magically produces a dove from a top hat, and strangles the dove; an American president is seen blasting a lump of butter with his gun and complaining, 'It's got no balls, butter,' while a Michael Foot puppet laments the economic depression afflicting his old friends in Ebbw Vale: 'my tailor, my barber, my embalmer, the man who used to saw the bottoms off old Seven-Up bottles to make my glasses – all unemployed'. It also had an imaginative sequence about a Japanese samurai winning a *hari-kiri* competition by slicing off the top of his head with a sword and then reaching for a grapefruit knife to work round the rim of his severed skull. He then added a glacé cherry and sliver of orange on a cock-tail stick to the contents of his skull before eating what remained of his head. This proved fatal to the samurai and very nearly extinguished his puppeteer. My favourite visual joke, however, was the improvised sequence in which one of President Reagan's loyal puppet aides reaches for the set builder's industrial stapler and re-attaches the President's slip-ping wig, back to front.

More important than what we liked, however, was that fact that Charles Denton, Central's Director of Programmes, was ecstatic about it. After watching the videotape of the pilot, Denton rang John Lloyd to say he wanted to give *Spitting Image* the big treatment – twenty-six continuous weekly shows. Lloyd, remembering how crippling a *Not the Nine O'Clock News* series of eight had been, begged for a smaller favour. Eventually they compromised on thirteen, and Denton, on reflection, was glad Lloyd had talked him out of the longer commitment. He was gladder still when the bills for the pilot came in.

We celebrated the success of the pilot with a party in the gar-den of Fluck's home in Duxford, inviting all the gilded people associated with the venture along with their families. Clive Sinclair, recently knighted, came by and wished us well. The sun also shone down on us as evidence of heavenly approval.

There was an agreeable sense of being on good terms with the world and on top of it at the same time. Everybody seemed quite wonderful, even the academic friend of Fluck's who sidled up and said, 'So, you've moved to the other side.'

'What do you mean?' asked Peter.

'Up to now,' said the friend, 'you've only been responsible for your own egos. Now you'll spend most of your life worrying about other people's.'

It cast a chill at the time, but only a very slight one. What really made the party was the fact that none of the *Spitting Image* children ever came out to play. They stayed indoors watching the video of the pilot, over and over again.

From then on it was all pretty much downhill. To accommodate our new venture we used Central's money to rent space in what had been a rum and banana warehouse amid the defunct cranes of London's West India Dock. This would be our new workshop. Ironically, our landlords there, Limehouse Studios, were blessed with studio facilities that would have enabled *Spitting Image* to be shot downstairs, but there was no possibility of anything that sensible being arranged. We were told the unions would not wear it.

We were sorry to leave the chapel, but it had hardly been big enough to cope with the R & D for *Spitting Image*, let alone the actual show. The move from the chapel to East London was accomplished in a pantechnicon loaned to us by Central Television. On arrival Fluck and I discovered that our twenty-five models, prototypes for the first puppets, each had a stick pointing out of the top of its head. They had been impaled with their own armatures. We knew exactly how they must feel.

In truth, though, when set beside the early days of *Spitting Image,* a hole in the head would have made a most refreshing experience. I remember those days as the worst period of my life. Peter Fluck has a similar recollection.

To be on the job at all hours we set up a working home in Star Lane, Canning Town, on the edge of a perfectly preserved bomb site. Hendra, Fluck and I lived there with our first workshop employee, Steve Bendelack. Like boxers in training for the big fight, we felt that that isolation from the distractions of family life was of the essence. And, like boxers, we became meaner with every passing day. Our evenings would be spent drinking together and infecting one another with pessimistic news from different parts of the battlefield. There was nothing to relieve the tension, and tension is one of the worst enemies of a sense of humour. This subsequently enabled Fluck to formulate one of his rules of existence – 'Those who are not getting on during the day, should not drink together in the evening' – but it was not much help at the time. We were quite literally terrified of our own show, with good reason.

We had taken five months preparing the pilot, grooming it lovingly all the while. Now we were confronted with having to make thirteen shows for delivery in successive weeks. This entailed a production schedule which laid down that, at any one time, three shows would be going through different phases of preparation. And just to simplify matters, Central had insisted that the shows be shot at their Birmingham studios. So our magnificent creations would be forever jolting up and down the M1, either *en route* to stardom or coming back for badly needed repairs.

The enormity of it all was compounded by an unfunny struggle between our funniest men. Hendra, the scripts supremo, and Lloyd, the show's producer, were locked in what seemed like an irreconcilable battle about what the puppets should say and how they should behave. Hendra was inclined to favour outrageous characters, like all Russians as bears for example, and for deploying them in regular mini sit-coms. He envisaged an 'old Prime Ministers Retirement Home' featuring the plentiful supply of redundant premiers around at that time – Macmillan, Wilson, Home, Heath and Callaghan – and an informal, wise-cracking Ayatollah Khomeni starring in a mosque sit-com – 'Hi Honey, I'm Home'. Lloyd made no secret of the fact that he found these ideas too cumbersome and restricting. He was more drawn to the idea of lookalike characters which he felt would provide more flexibility, and he saw them operating most effectively in short, sharp sketches. Nobody was particularly happy with the compromises that had to be made.

It is probably true to say that none of us actually liked the first *Spitting Image* show which was transmitted in February 1984. However, in hindsight, some of the visual gags were quite good, achieving a high level of profoundly bad taste. We had our Ronald Reagan inquiring of Nancy if the earth moved for her in a bedroom scene and, on receiving a negative, pressing the button marked 'Nuke'; our Mick Jagger bending over a milk shake, and sniffing it through the straw; and our Colonel Gaddafi opening the brown envelope containing the Terrorist of the Year nominations, and blowing himself up. We were all sore, however, at having lost the star of our show. Peter Harris, our *Muppets*-turned-*Spitting Image* director, had predicted that the Queen would triumphantly emerge as 'our Miss Piggy'. But the board of Central Television had ruled that she should not appear so as not to embarrass Prince Philip, who was due to open the company's Nottingham studio the following week.

In fact, the censored material was tame in comparison to

what came later. For the record, it revolved around the attempts of Mrs Thatcher to obtain an audience with the Queen who was intent on frying sausages and watching TV. Eventually the Queen relents and enters the audience chamber where Mrs Thatcher dutifully rises.

Queen: Why Mrs Thatcher. Do sit down.
Thatcher sits down.
Queen: Do stand up.
Thatcher stands up.
Queen: Do sit down.
Thatcher sits down.
Queen: Do stand up.
Thatcher [*annoyed*]: Is this protocol, Ma'am?
Queen: No, no. It's just fun being Queen.

The thing that was most distressing about the first show, at least for Fluck and myself, was how appalling our caricatures looked. The crude glare of the television lights seemed to maximize their every defect in a way that was truly cringe-making for us both. It was as if the hours we had spent with John Lawrence Jones getting our models lit to best effect had been for nothing. It being television, we felt we were more likely to be judged on how these characters looked, and to our eyes they looked terrible. This aggravation would lead to one of the more famous exchanges on the studio floor, when Fluck, totally usurping the lighting director's authority, commanded, 'Turn out half the lights.' 'Which half?' came the subtle reply, but Fluck – not about to be blinded by science – roared back, 'Any half.'

With every day that passed Fluck and I were becoming more

acquainted with 'the other side', as his academic pal had put it – constantly having to navigate our way through a thicket of other people's egos in order to get, very occasionally, our own way. The problem in Birmingham, according to Fluck, was that we did not know what we were doing and they did not know what had hit them. When *Spitting Image* was being filmed the studio floor, accustomed for twenty years to the stately measures of *Crossroads*, would look like a cross between a madhouse and a slaughterhouse. There would be heads and bits of bodies all over the shop and puppeteers on the verge of dementia trying to synchronize awkward latex mouths with pre-recorded in-character voices. There would be amazing creatures with six legs preening themselves in front of mirrors which, on closer inspection, would be revealed as three puppeteers rehearsing a single puppet character, one operating the head and an arm, one operating the other arm, and one working the eye movement.

While all this incredibly chaotic and un-*Crossroads*-like activity was going on and causing upset in the studio, the men in suits were coming up with some alarming calculations. Our modest original idea had grown to the extent of becoming the most expensive comedy show on television (the first series cost well over £2 million) and, by a million miles, the slowest to produce. It would take one hour of studio time, television's most sacred commodity, to produce one screenable minute of *Spitting Image*. Fluck's suggestion of retitling the show *The Enough Money for a Mental Hospital Show* was not regarded as very funny.

In television terms there had never been a beast quite like it. One of the paradoxes of *Spitting Image* was that while it was a wholly original show, it contained virtually nothing that was new. Practically all the elements were as old as either Punch and Judy or John Logie Baird's invention of 'seeing with wireless'. The historical first was assembling a cast of puppeteers, costumiers, voice impressionists, mould makers, TV cameramen, foam experts, set-builders, funny writers, model-makers from the Fens and electricians recently made redundant from the motor industry, and expecting them to work harmoniously together, without any previous experience of so doing. Eventfully, some degree of harmony would be achieved, but there would be precious little in the early stages. John Lloyd would describe the task of producing the whole works as 'like pulling a dinosaur backwards by its tail'.

Law and Fluck

CHAPTER TEN

HiT AND MiSS

It was twelve years from *Spitting Image*'s first show until it finally came off air (1984–96). Although it might seem like a period to be cherished, as the summit of achievement for Fluck and myself, this was not the case. For the most part the experience of actually realizing the dream of bringing our caricatures to life seemed like one adrenalin-charged hassle after another, with precious little relief. We soon came to appreciate that our true function in the enterprise we had so incautiously created was to double up as its slaves and its slave-drivers.

I do not propose now to relive the whole gruelling experience blow by blow. Keen students of the history of satire can find all the dates they need in the British Newspaper Library at Colindale as *Spitting Image* was, episode by episode, the most thoroughly reported show of its time, particularly in the tabloids. But there are some memories, even painful ones, that I can bear to call to mind. The most vivid of them is of the show's first impact on the national press. On balance, they thought it stank.

My old newspapers led the assault. The *Observer* thought our initial effort was 'a dog', while the *Sunday Times*, mildly more charitable, described it as 'slow' and in need of a radical shake-up. Since Fluck and I had spent almost our entire working lives trying to beguile editors in what is termed the quality press, this was something of a shock to the system. It was even more of a shock to find ourselves eagerly scouring the columns of the *Sun* and the *Star*, where some of the earliest crumbs of comfort to *Spitting Image* were to be found.

At *Spitting Image* we never made the seasoned actor's pretence of paying no attention to reviews. This was because it was very difficult for anyone who worked on the show to actually see it as a whole. All people could see was how their own specialism had been violated. Puppeteers would rage about camera angles allowing their elbows to appear in shot, writers would get nasty about the mutilation of their punch lines, while the model-makers would rage against the lighting. For an objective view of what the show was actually like we were pathetically dependent on the press, at least in the early days. Later I came to realize that punditry on satire is a bit like football reporting. Even the most hopelessly unathletic scribe can tell the England manager exactly where he is going wrong, and similarly even the most humourless broadsheet columnist is an expert on how satire has totally gone off the rails since the days of Jonathan Swift. But it was some time before I arrived at this comforting perception.

We did not really generate any confidence in our own judgement until we were almost half way through the first series. By that time the internal war over how the puppets should behave had been resolved, with John Lloyd emerging as the victor, and Hendra returning, defeated, to the United States. There was no rejoicing in this, but it was a relief to have the struggle over and done with. With Lloyd in unfettered charge of production the emphasis was much more on sharper sketches, higher puppet turnover and increased topicality. Last-minute changes, to accommodate the latest news, became the order of the day. All of this implied a much higher workload for Fluck and myself and the team of youngsters – most of them fresh out of art school – we had slaving in the workshop. There was naturally some friction on this score. But the truly irritating thing about Lloyd, aside from his talent, charm, wit, blond good looks and bedroom blue eyes, was the fact that he was usually right.

From the outset it was agreed that I would run the workshop while Fluck would ingratiate himself with the natives and whisper warnings in my ear if they seemed to be getting restless. They rarely seemed to be getting anything else. They called the show *Splitting Headache*. We started out with a workshop staff of eleven, sufficient we thought to cater for all the puppet-making processes – research (into what the characters looked like in real life), drawing, modelling, moulding, foaming (as we moved from little latex characters to big, fleshy, foamy ones), fitting (of eyes and special features, like revolving toupees) and costume. We reckoned to get an individual puppet through all these processes in a week. With camels, sheep and lizards and sparsely dressed puppets like Michael Heseltine as Tarzan, we could perhaps knock off a couple of days.

As the pace quickened to cope with John Lloyd's insatiable

appetite for new heads, the work automatically became more specialized and streamlined. Very few caricaturists take a great interest in the neck, but a good neck is vital to the happiness of a puppeteer. You really could not ask the high-grade child labour at our disposal to treat this as a high-priority problem, so my own working days would be devoted to producing high-speed necks, in much the same way as my father had once laid high-speed bricks. Sadly my father had died shortly before *Spitting Image* was created without realizing how close our destinies would become.

Fluck would describe our working life as like being on the assembly line at Fords after being trained to hand-make cars at Rolls Royce. But it still needed a lot of ingenuity to overcome the fresh problems that kept cropping up, and most of it was supplied by Fluck. Without real problems to solve, Fluck was inclined to regress into the reinvention of useful objects like the wheel, but there was rarely time for such diversions at *Spitting Image*. He went into the first series as the esteemed inventor of the eye movement – a cheap brass and cable arrangements that worked far better than the £800 contraption on offer from the film industry – and came out of it as the hero of numerous other solutions that were both low tech and highly practical.

Another Fluck contribution was to scale down the mechanisms behind the bridge of the puppet's nose, which allowed us to get eyes closer together and thus inject a much shiftier look. When the puppeteers, angered by the difficulty of keeping their handholds, threatened mutiny, it was Fluck who saved the day again with a visit to the stationers. He thought that fingerstalls at the end of their handgrips might be the answer, and they were. Later we found these same fingerstalls were excellently suited for the modelling of pitted flesh, which gave greater verisimilitude to characters like General Noriega and Richard Ingrams.

Another intriguing discovery was that there is an iconography of famous heads we all carry around with us, and it relates more to a head's overall shape than anything else. This probably also explains why it is pointless to caricature people who are not famous. Since we have no generalized preconceived image of how they look, there can, outside friends and family, be no jolt of recognition that has to be the largest ingredient of success in any caricature. This probably also ties in with recent medical research that suggests babies recognize their mothers not by their facial features but through an awareness of the shape of their heads. A mother, after all, is usually baby's first famous person.

We increasingly found that the measure of a successful puppet depended on how well we captured the overall shape of a head. This was why the 'roughing out' stage – making the bold shape – ranked at least equal in importance to all the telling little disfigurements. We were particularly pleased with our John Major because we felt that we got the iconography of his unusual cranium exactly right, though he was also esteemed, later when he became Prime Minister, for his ability to use up our huge surplus supplies of grey emulsion paint.

Despite this level of discovery and invention there was always a sense in the workshop of being at the exploited end of the enterprise. It would be Lloyd and his team of writers who set the pace, and we would be forever struggling to keep up. As a deadline loomed, Lloyd would give me a list of puppet characters that had to be made yesterday, often with no clue as to how they might be used in the show. I remember we crafted a brilliant Pavarotti with a small head to emphasize his gigantic

Pablo Bach

girth, only later to discover that the gag was for him to swallow four telephones and a 12 foot omelette. This would require a brand new Luciano Pavarotti, only achieved by working through the night.

Fluck and I also found ourselves losing any real grip on things outside the workshop. Our original idea was that the show should be almost entirely politics, and as radical as we could manage without being obvious. To this end the Queen was conceived as a sort of benevolent Marxist who had to endure the insufferable woman who happened to be the Prime Minister. Despite this felicitous invention, it became clear, especially as John Lloyd grew in confidence, that politics was being edged to one side. We had some vigorous debates on this subject in Birmingham, during one of which I was alleged to have tried to strangle him, though I was only feeling the quality of the lapels on his jacket.

The Lloyd argument, in brief, was that politics simply could not sustain the show, especially now that an attempt was being made to make it as snappy as possible. We all knew that when the puppets trotted on the screen the initial suspension of disbelief was colossal, after which it went very rapidly downhill. This was because puppets are lousy actors and, being legless, even worse dancers. Aside from popping up and bonking each other on the head, there was nothing they could do of themselves that was intrinsically funny. The only way to disguise their ineptness was to keep the jokes coming thick and fast. The problem was that putting good jokes into the mouths of characters with only a limited range of expression required exceptionally good joke-writers. Writers of this quality were rare, and some of them had no interest in politics whatsoever. But if the show was to survive it would have to corral these writers and give them scope. And that inevitably meant broadening the show out beyond politics and into the areas of media and entertainment and beyond.

We very reluctantly bought the argument as far as entertainment figures were concerned, but when requests for sports stars started coming down, the workshop played merry hell. This, it was argued, was like being asked to caricature people for no better reason than that they were there. But somehow Steve 'Very Interesting' Davis got made and a few others managed to squeeze through the manufacturing process over my live, quivering body. Then I met up with my old patron Peter Cook, after an intermission of twenty-three years, and he told me that the thing he liked most about *Spitting Image* was the way it sent up the sports stars. The political satire left him unmoved. 'If I want to know about politics,' said Cook, 'I'll read the papers.'

From the second series onwards we achieved a rough balance of 50 per cent political material and 50 per cent media, entertainment and sport, which gave the writers something broader to work with. Originally Ian Hislop and Nick Newman from *Private Eye* provided most of the sharp political stuff while Rob Grant and Doug Naylor, who would go on to fashion *Red Dwarf*, provided what became one of *Spitting Image*'s richest ingredients – silliness. My personal favourite *Spitting Image* sketch of all time was a Grant–Naylor conception involving the Gielgud and Olivier puppets contemplating old acquaintances, all 'gone, goney, gone'.

There was a lot of luck involved in whether a caricature worked well as a puppet. It helped if a character had a big mouth, as this made it much easier for the puppeteer to do his or her job. The Queen's puppet benefited enormously from being based on a caricature with a big mouth, as did the Walter

Matthau and Ian Paisley puppets. A consequence of Mrs Thatcher's having a small, tight mouth was that her puppet was always difficult to manipulate. Since we could not take the liberty of dispensing big mouths to all and sundry, it just became a discomfort we all had to live with.

There were, however, certain areas in which we were prepared to adjust reality. It has been said that time is the best caricaturist, but this is not always the case. In her old films, Lauren Bacall really did have extraordinary cat's eyes, ones that turned sharply up, but by the time we got round to modelling her they had turned the other way. With characters like Bacall, and to some extent Laurence Olivier, we would compromise the caricature to include a large element of how people remembered they looked, rather than how they actually did look, for the sake of credibility on the screen.

It might be thought that after so many compromises of our political and aesthetic outlook, Fluck and I should have lost all stomach with the enterprise. 'What on earth are we doing here?' did become a kind of catchphrase of our partnership, but on my side it was a joke and it usually, though not invariably, was with Fluck. Despite all the frustrations, there was always the sense of participating in something quite extraordinary. It might not be the acme of caricature or the most hard-edged political satire but it still seemed like a creation worth persevering with. And many of our conflicts had not been so much over principle, as coming to an understanding of what the creation could do and what it couldn't. There being no real precedent for the show, there were no wise old geezers around capable of proffering us useful advice. Everything had to be learned the hard way.

Ultimately, we knew we had no reason to blame John Lloyd,

or indeed anybody else, for the fact the *Spitting Image* never managed to achieve a real political cutting edge. Nor could we even blame the requirement for 'balance' on television. In practice, the show tended to balance itself as part of the relentless quest for characters who could make it work. This automatically meant that none of the leading politicians in the Opposition could be left unmolested. Mrs Thatcher and the crazed Michael Heseltine were probably the two most popular political characters in the show for many years, but they were closely followed by Neil Kinnock as Kinnocchio, Roy Hattersley as a spitting machine and David Steel as a babe cradled in the arms of a satanic David Owen.

We were also surprised at the degree to which caricature combined with puppetry proved not so much savage as endearing. Politicians were often discomforted by their puppet images, but they did represent membership of a weird kind of popular elect. It was probably more discomforting for them when their images ceased to appear.

Central Television would deliver a tape of the show to the House of Commons on Monday mornings for Members who had missed it the night before. We were reliably informed that junior members of the Cabinet (and Shadow Cabinet) were absolutely delighted when their puppets appeared. It showed they were on their way up. This had to be a triumph of ambition over personal sensitivity as we tried hard not to depict them at their very best. The puppets on the show were supposed to act as we imagined their human doppelgängers behaved off-camera in private, with their hair let down. We did not always get this right, as it was sometimes hard for even our lurid imaginations to keep pace with reality. Our Edwina Currie puppet debuted as Cruella de Ville though, with hindsight, we should have had her bonking the puppet John Major.

Gillray and Cruikshank, our caricaturist heroes, had usefully supplemented their incomes by selling off their original plates to politicians tired of being lampooned. When I suggested that we might apply this principle by selling off our puppets in the same way, and thus finance our escape from *Spitting Image,* Fluck could not have been more dismissive. 'Never work,' he said. 'They couldn't bear not to see themselves on the show next week.'

The truth of that matter is that it really is very hard to offend public figures when satire is in vogue. We picked on the Tory politician Leon Brittain's rather poor complexion, cruelly highlighting his facial spots. Not long afterwards, John Lloyd was sampling the dips at a West End function when Mrs Leon Brittain came over to him and hissed in his ear, 'I love Leon's puppet, but not enough spots.' Michael Heseltine reported that his wild-eyed, demented puppet gave him a hero's status with his own children; previously they had just regarded him as a boring old Cabinet Minister. I think it is just possible that we offended Mrs Thatcher, but she was far too bright to admit it. She never watched the show, it was alleged.

Non-political celebrities were also quite hard to offend, though to be fair Paul Daniels, whose puppet sported a revolving toupee, Andrew Lloyd Webber, whose puppet washed his hair in baked beans, and Claire Rayner, whose puppet was a bit on the ample side, all thought we were thoroughly detestable. But they were exceptions, not the rule. I think we stumbled on what is now a widely appreciated phenomenon as a consequence of seeing so many famous people voluntarily making prats of themselves on *Big Brother*-type shows. For many celebrities no humiliation is too great if it affords the chance of being noticed.

The Royals came in a slightly different category, mainly because – as we were constantly told – they could not defend themselves, though this hardly seemed necessary as there were so many passionate defenders ready to give voice on their behalf. But the experience of losing the Queen in our first transmission did encourage us to proceed with some caution. I can remember Lloyd flatly refusing to entertain a workshop idea that we should introduce the Queen Mother puppet by having her win an arm-wrestling competition with her younger daughter with a slug of gin at stake. Eventually, Lloyd introduced the Queen Mum puppet deftly by having her pop up after the final credits had rolled to say how disappointed she was not to have been in the show. This episode yielded our all-time top viewing figure of 11.4 million, though it had been a shade over-promoted. In anticipation of the Queen Mother caricature the *Daily Express* had got us off to a magnificent start by instructing all its readers to switch off in protest against 'squalid backroom boys who hide snide and shallow jokes behind their sniggering puppet faces'. Naturally, they all switched on.

From then on we had no real problems with the Royals, who became one of the show's more enduring mini sit-coms. Our treatment of them was robust, but I like to think that we never lowered the tone of the monarchy quite as far as Rupert Murdoch's *Sun*. Ultimately of course nobody lowered the tone quite as efficiently as the Royals themselves.

One thing that militated against a consistent radical line on the Royals, or indeed anything else, was the fact that the show was made with the direct input of literally scores of people – ranging from devout monarchists to hard-line Marxists – who would be quite unable to agree the political time of day among themselves. It is also possible that I was more of a traditionalist than I originally gave myself credit for. I had some inkling of this when my son Shem borrowed my suit for his first big job interview. The consequence was that the same suit worked at the *Observer* again after an interval of several years. In some obscure, dynastic way I found this deeply pleasing.

I cannot honestly say we suffered much from censorship, at least after our initial problem with the Queen. Aside from very small disappointments, like the Broadcasting Authority banning a Bernard Levin sketch in which his puppet explained why he became a writer – 'I think it was because I was circumcised with a pencil sharpener' – most of what we considered our most outrageous material was transmitted.

Indeed, Fluck and I, after years of having to negotiate our grotesques into print, were both astonished by how much it was possible to get away with on television. The week Reagan bombed Libya with Mrs Thatcher's approval, we did a sketch based on *One Man and His Dog*. This featured the puppet Reagan as a shepherd with Mrs Thatcher as a poodle jumping through hoops before finally licking her master's bottom. It aroused very little comment, but when we tried to publish the final image on the cover of a *Spitting Image* book the lawyers went ballistic. We could be as rude as rude on TV, but not in print. The same went for bloodthirsty, though our most savage offering in this area actually came from outside the workshop. The advertising team who had penned 'You'll never get a better bit of butter on your knife' created a sequence, with our technical assistance, that featured an effigy of the South African premier, P.W. Botha, sitting at his desk, prior to being sliced into numerous small pieces by three puppet freedom-fighters,

Reagan and Thatcher

who then went on to harmonize, 'You'll never get a better bit of Botha on your knife.'

I'm still not quite sure why we enjoyed such latitude in these areas, but I think the ephemeral nature of television had a lot to do with it. That, and the fact that the English only seem to take two things seriously, gardening and literature. As for the box – 'it's only television'.

People sometimes ask me what was the secret of *Spitting Image*'s success, and I am inclined to think it was sheer luck. To perform satirical tricks effectively you have to be around at the right time, with the right people. James Gillray, back in the late eighteenth century, had Pitt and Napoleon and a robust decade obsessed with money and celebrity as his targets. *Spitting Image* was blessed with Thatcher and Reagan and another robust decade obsessed with money and celebrity.

John Lloyd has the theory that we actually helped Mrs Thatcher stay in power by acting as a 'safety valve'. As he put it, 'We showed her being knocked about, dressed up like a vampire and generally made a fool of, and people said, ' "Thank God someone is saying what is going on," so they didn't take to the streets.' As I have not yet received a formal 'Thank You' letter from Mrs Thatcher for all my efforts on her behalf, I'm not prepared to go all the way with this analysis, but there is no question that when Mrs Thatcher and Ronald Reagan departed from high office a bright light of motivation went out of our lives.

While the show's insights may have been too diffuse to have much influence on how people voted, I think it undoubtedly did influence perceptions, especially after the newspapers took to illustrating their regular feature articles with stills from *Spitting Image*. I can remember after the 1987 election leafing through a set of photographs of the new Tory Cabinet in one of the Sunday papers, and asking Deirdre if she had seen them. She replied, 'That's not photographs of them, you idiot. They're photographs of your puppets.' And over the years I've noticed with delight that many other people acquired a tendency to confuse the caricature with the real person. If you ask me what effect the show had, I would say it helped to create a little more disrespect for people in high places, which was probably no bad thing.

One thing it certainly helped to create was a lot of interesting career structures. Because it was such a high-pressure operation, those who managed to cope with its lunacies and implacable deadlines tended to do well in their subsequent ventures. This was particularly true of our 'voices' – the people we recruited to give our caricatures the power of speech. I can remember an engaging young character called Harry Enfield hanging around the workbench and bending our ears by giving us a fresh slant on the Bible – Jesus, he insisted, was born in Bethnal Green not Bethlehem. In order to get some work done, we persuaded Lloyd to take him on as 'a voice', which subsequently led to higher things. Other *Spitting Image* 'voices' who did rather well for us, and not too badly for themselves, were Rory Bremner, Chris Barrie, Steve Coogan, Alistair McGowan and our imperishable 'Mrs Thatcher', Steven Nallon.

In the workshop two of our child-labourers, Tim Watts and David Stoten, emerged as caricaturists of great distinction, far outstripping their original mentors. Our first workshop employee, Steve Bendelack, was lost to the workbench, though happily not the enterprise, as soon as he got his eye behind a camera. Bendelack became our ace at producing special effects with video. Puppets became capable of morphing into insects and flying away, while a few camera passes over a dozen puppets could, under his influence, become a Nuremberg rally in post-production. Bendelack also managed to seamlessly marry puppets shot on video with stop-motion shot on film which, in case anyone is still wondering, was how we managed to get Robert Maxwell as King Midas turning everything he touched into a common waste product. In his post-*Spitting Image* incarnation Bendelack became a pivotal comedy director (*The Royle Family*, *League of Gentlemen* and *Little Britain*).

John Lloyd also moved on to further Bafta award-winning triumphs with *Blackadder*, before taking a long, well-deserved and well-heeled rest. Giles Pilbrow, one of Lloyd's successors as producer, would later imaginatively take advantage of the animation opportunities provided by the new computer technology. His successful satirical cartoon show, *2D-TV,* would eventually take up residence in *Spitting Image*'s old slot – 10 o'clock on Sunday night. Yet another *Spitting Image* producer was Bill Dare, whose aversion to puppets after a while came to match my own. He also progressed in an interesting way. Years later I was invited to watch the pilot for his new programme, *Dead Ringers*. Afterwards in the bar I ventured to point out that *Dead Ringers* had much in common with *Spitting Image*, to which Dare replied, 'It's exactly the same except at last I've got rid of the fucking puppets.'

During the last few series of *Spitting Image* I'm bound to confess that I used every excuse I could muster to absent myself from the workbench, which, incidentally, was no great loss as it was now staffed by people whose competence far exceeded mine. However, there was a serious outbreak of frivolity in my absence. A caricature puppet of me was made and inserted into the show at different times in a variety of unflattering guises – as a bug-eyed lunatic artist, a bull-necked white South African racist, and the legless drunk whom Princess Diana rescued from drowning in St James's Park. I must say I did find the distorted image of myself on the screen faintly disturbing, but of course one had to laugh.

In retrospect, the experience of assembling the *Spitting Image* programmes was not one I would have missed, but I could have stood the strain of its being much less prolonged. And when, four years after the last show, I was offered a huge pile of money to put it all back together again, I was able say with heartfelt conviction: 'You must be joking.'

CHAPTER ELEVEN

SPITTING IMPERIALISM

Producing satirical puppets to order is probably a shade more interesting than canning peas, but after a while it too can get monotonous. So when areas of opportunity arose that would allow me to absent myself from the production line, I tended to take them eagerly. One such area was Spitting Imperialism, which often involved travel and the chance to get to know nutty people of many different cultures and creeds, usually at their expense. It was also quite good for business. The funds earned through franchise and consultancy deals with other nations helped sustain the money-guzzling British operation.

In truth, though I call it Imperialism, we rarely actually sought cultural conquest. As the British Empire evolved naturally as a consequence of the dominance of the British Navy, ours, equally naturally, proceeded from our dominance in satirical puppet design. By the late 1980s requests for help in setting up *Spitting Image*-style shows were pouring in from all corners of Europe, and way beyond. Historically it was clear that our moment had arrived. As luck would have it the rise of *Spitting Image* coincided almost exactly with collapse of international Communism, and no new democracy, it seemed, felt fully equipped without its very own satirical puppet show.

Among the first petitioners to arrive at our London studios was an energetic young entrepreneur from Prague. He told me that the first time he saw a tape of *Spitting Image* he vowed to make a similar show in the Czech Republic once the Communist regime had crumbled – which it just had. We agreed terms on the same day, making arrangements for his team to come to London for training. I was, however, obliged to confess that I had a delegation of Russian satirists booked in at roughly the same time. 'Never mind,' he said. 'We put up with the Russians for forty years – what's a few days more?'

Perhaps fortunately, the Russians, reliably unpunctual as ever, failed to show. So the Czechs got our undivided attention. Their actual show, *Gumaci*, was put together in an old cinema in the gypsy quarter of Prague, to which I was subsequently invited. *Gumaci* had already shot up to third in the ratings, and they were celebrating a call from the Castle complaining about their portrayal of the head of state as 'stupid'. The implication was that they could characterize Vaclav Havel any way they liked, but stupid – no. I would count the Czechs as being among our most adept students, though I thought their satire could have a little more edge. I was amused to notice that they had even picked up on one of our trade secrets, which was: when short of material, run a weatherman sketch.

146

The Hungarian initiative was no less impressive, but in a different way. I was first approached by Miklos Salusinszky, a lone Hungarian pleading poverty coupled with unbridled admiration for our enterprise. Feeling charitable, I showed him all the processes for free, and he went back to Budapest and fashioned his own show, *Uborka*, which rapidly built up an audience of more than 4 million viewers out of a potential 10 million. I was invited to see it. While watching the show-reel at his studio, I was taken aback by the extraordinary realism of his set, replicating the interior of the Hungarian Parliament. How come we hadn't been paid, I asked Miklos, when he could afford such expensive sets? The answer was that they filmed all the political stuff actually in the Parliament. This was some achievement. Filming puppets on location can be incredibly hazardous as it is so hard to screen out the puppeteers. The Hungarians did it with hand-held cameras and puppeteers manoeuvring on skateboards – something we had never tried. Again, I thought the satire a little on the mild side, though this was perhaps inevitable given who owned the set. The producer took the point, but countered, 'You British have been cutting the grass for 400 years. We Hungarians have only been doing it for four.' Besides which, money was still in short supply. They could only do the show through the winter because their cartoonist spent his summers in Hosok Tere (the main square), where he could earn more drawing tourists.

The Bulgarians had a satire show called *Coo Coo* which, as it only featured one puppet, was never going to provide us with much of an outlet. One day, however, I got a call from *Private Eye* to say that Nelly Andreeva, the producer of *Coo Coo*, was in town, that she seemed a very interesting lady and that she was eager to have a cultural exchange with *Spitting Image*. I was not expecting much from the encounter, but it was a good enough excuse to vacate the work bench. So I headed over to Greek Street, and I was very glad I did. The main item of interest proved be a tape of a couple of sketches from her show, which had nothing to do with puppets, but a lot to do with satire.

In the first, a black news reporter appeared on the screen outside the Bulgarian Parliament. As eminent MPs left the building the news reporter introduced himself, saying he was from Utamba in Africa, and asking if they would like to comment on the troubled situation in that country. He then raised the microphone for their response. Each politician managed to come up with a resourceful, and solicitous, exposition on his party's position on Utamba, which of course did not exist. The final frame had the 'reporter', nose to camera, confiding that he was really an exchange student from Zimbabwe. It was a wickedly funny piss-take of a type I'd not seen done before, though the technique would later become familiar when a comedian called Ali G appeared on the scene.

The other Bulgarian sketch featured another fake reporter interviewing a very real military police guard outside a nuclear power station. 'Tell me,' asked the reporter, 'is it true that you have a meltdown inside the power station?' The military policeman's look of genuine horror was more than enough to undermine his formal denial of any problem. This particular item, I was told, had caused a panic across Bulgaria and Romania: roads were blocked by fleeing cars in scenes reminiscent of those brought about by Orson Welles's famous radio broadcast *War of the Worlds*. After our meeting Nelly demurely trotted back to Bulgaria, with me thinking perhaps we should go to her for lessons.

The Germans, initially, were a big disappointment. They came to see us at our workshop to say that they wanted a wide range of puppets made for a comedy show. They emphasized that the show they envisaged would not offend anyone and would be in no way satirical. As we rather haughtily thought of satire as being the main point of the enterprise, we sent them back to Germany with no puppets and only a modicum of advice. Subsequently they did their own thing, producing a puppet show called *Gum*, which started off in timorous vein but eventually became uproariously savage. The dramatic change in the show had nothing whatsoever to do with our input. It was essentially a response to the expanded audience created through Germany's reunification. The East Germans, it transpired, adored the puppets particularly when they were behaving really badly. So the show's producer adroitly adjusted it to suit their taste. I remember watching one of the later shows with intense admiration. It featured a pastiche of the German movie *Das Boot*, with the entire German puppet government sitting in a U-boat being depth-charged. Really most effective.

The Italians were very nice to deal with. We made puppets to order for their projected new show, *Teste di Gomma*. They paid us on time and were refreshingly open to our ideas, though they politely rejected my notion of a mini sit-com involving the Pope and one of Italy's leading Mafia-linked politicians. After such an agreeable start to our collaboration, I was mortified to read that the Italian government had resigned *en masse* only a few days before the Italian show was due to go on air. I rang their producer to commiserate over what seemed like a disaster – all the puppets we had made were of politicians in the now fallen government. But for him it was 'no problemo'. He explained that as all the same politicians would re-emerge, but in different jobs, the show could still be topical with only minor adjustment.

The Greeks came by with promises of money, and a deal was struck. To guide them through the early stages I visited their studios, a rather insanitary experience. It was located in a near-derelict warehouse in a suburb of Athens next to a huge olive-oil processing plant and a sluggish slick of evil-smelling pollution which might have been a river. The Greeks were great individualists and great improvisers, though their puppeteers all seemed a little bleary-eyed. I later learned that they all worked as security guards by night. The main voice artist for the show was inconveniently doing his national service at the time. So we wound up doing many of the recordings in an army barracks. Given the eccentric nature of the enterprise, I half feared that there might be some problems about liberating the money for our services, but things in this area improved immensely after we enlisted the help of a street-wise Athenian lawyer called Aristotle. Like the Italians, the Greeks experienced 'regime change' complications before their first transmission. The government called a snap election, and lost it to Andreas Papandreou. Our puppets of course were all caricatures of the outgoing administration, and most of them were unlikely to be back for some time at least. Unfazed, the Greek writers put together a show revealing what the previous government would have done had they won the election and stayed in office.

Turkey also ordered a consignment of puppets, and I went to Istanbul to see how things were developing. My situation there was relatively privileged, at least compared to Greece. I was wined and dined at a restaurant with a magnificent view across the Bosporus, but there was a palpable air of tension about the place, and about the puppet project. When I asked my host, who lived in a beautiful villa along the bay, he responded with a tight-lipped, 'You really don't want to know.' I was further unnerved when I was invited to inspect the main set for the projected show. This was a representation of the interior of a luxurious harem around which, in placard form, could be seen holy inscriptions from the Koran. Even I thought this was pushing it a bit. I left town with the money for the puppets, but I never did any follow-up on the show. I do not think it lasted very long.

Portugal, in contrast, was a delight. In Lisbon I dealt with Mandala Productions, which was headed by a formidable operator called Mafalda Mendes de Almeida, a woman with a past. In an earlier incarnation back in the mid-1970s she had been the Minister of Propaganda for the popular movement, and known as 'the spirit of the revolution'. She was the person responsible for getting *Battleship Potemkin* put on in the main cinema when I was covering the revolution for the *Sunday Times*. It was through one of Mafalda's introductions that I got to meet again the (then) young man who had been most helpful to me when I was reporting the revolution. It turned out that he was (now) the Minister of Culture in the Portuguese government. With friends like this you might imagine we wouldn't experience any problems in Portugal. In fact, Mafalda's first production with our puppets somehow failed to catch on, and rapidly came off air. But we all tried again a couple of years later, and this time the formula was right. The show just soared up the ratings and is still on air.

My attention was directed to Japan by Murray Sayle, the former *Sunday Times* correspondent who had moved to Tokyo where he wrote about Asian politics. Sayle maintained that the time was right for a Japanese *Spitting Image*, as never before had so much sincerity been shown by Japanese politicians – 'showing sincerity' being a euphemism for money changing hands.

I was myself a bit sceptical, for slightly dishonourable reasons. In our very first *Spitting Image* programme – the pilot which preceded the first show on air – we had unashamedly exploited stereotyped perceptions, or misperceptions, of the Japanese. The relevant sketch started with one Japanese puppet interviewing five other identical Japanese puppets to ascertain which should be the new Ambassador to the United States. The interviewer explained that they had all been chosen for their individuality because 'the hideous Yankee long-pigs seem to have the ridiculous notion that we all look the same to them'. The scripted exchanges between the puppets then proceeded on fairly predictable lines:

Two: I would like to nominate Mr Taizo Watanabe.
One: Well spoken, Mr Funakoshi.
Three: I haven't said anything yet.
Four: No need to apologize to me.
One: You are Mr Saka.
Five: No, I am Mr Saka.
One: So sorry, Mr Saka. I mistook you for Mr Funakoshi.
Four: No need to apologize.
One: Sorry? You are Mr Saka, then?
Four: No, I am Mr Funakoshi.
Three: Well, who the hell am I then?

Fortunately for our Far Eastern relations this sketch never appeared on public television, and Nippon duly joined our queue of interested customers. We sent Steve Bendelack, the director, and Richard Bennett, our financial director, over to Tokyo to teach them the tricks of the trade. They came back exhausted but deeply impressed. The exhaustion had apparently been occasioned by their having to work for thirty-six hours straight after getting off the plane. Later they discovered that their hosts had only indulged in this massive workathon out of politeness to their guests, whom they thought were keen to get on. In reality they too had been desperate for a kip. Bendelack brought back a tape of their first show, which was remarkable, not so much for its satire, but for the extraordinary dexterity of the puppeteers, superior to anything we achieved in our first year.

Before my advance on Moscow I had been told about the nature of the new Russian capitalism as defined by the writer Victor Pelevín. The procedure, he claimed, for budding capitalists was relatively simple: go to the bank, borrow a load of money, buy a 4-wheel drive, a fax machine and a crate of vodka. Then go home, drink the vodka, crash the 4-wheel drive and vomit over the fax machine. Then repeat the sequence as before. Then go to the bank a third time, learning *en route* that it has been taken over by the Mafia. Borrow another load of money, buy a gun and shoot yourself.

So I was forewarned.

We, Richard Bennett and I, arrived in the Russian capital during Boris Yeltsin's honeymoon with his people. No one seemed to be remotely in control. While we were there a gang seized the equivalent of £8 million from one of the banks, and returned the money the same afternoon. Even the criminal classes were in a state of chronic uncertainty. Indecision was also the main characteristic of our discussions, though there was no shortage of large promises. We were told that the audience for our puppets could on cold nights, which were exceptionally frequent in those parts, reach up to 350 million people. The potential had no limit. But nothing, in practical terms, ever seemed to get pinned down. Meantime the vodka kept flowing, if anything slightly faster than the Volga. As I was inconveniently on the wagon at the time, I would vainly ask for something non-alcoholic. 'But of course,' they'd say. 'Bring some beer for our English friend.'

We did eventually reach an agreement of sorts with a newly independent production company called 'Authors TV' (ATV). This pledged us to teaching the Russians how to make the puppets and set up their show, which was to be called *Rubber Souls*, a play on the title of Gogol's book *Dead Souls*. In their turn the Russians agreed to form a company to steer the enterprise, in which *Spitting Image* had a 25 per cent share. On our return to London we flourished the scrap of paper outlining the agreement before our grim-faced managing director, Joanna Beresford. 'Great,' she intoned. 'So you've got 25 per cent of nothing.'

Events were to prove she was not far off the mark, though the Russians kept in close touch, undertaking to send 'probationers' to London to acquire our arcane skills. Again there were complications of a deeply obscure nature. Shortly before one of their scheduled visits I received the following fax from Moscow:

'To our great misfortune the situation with the project *Rubber Souls* turned out to be a detective story. The person who was in charge for organizing the probationer's trip to London committed sabotage by some unknown reasons (which are going to be clarified by the specialists). Judging by the fact that there was no objective reasons for this and we didn't doubt qualification and decentness of the employee until recent, so we only may propose an intellectual spying ... Hoping that soon we shall be able to receive explanation of the accident we expect your understanding ...'

I never did manage to clarify the *Rubber Souls* spy drama but it was clear that the Russians were not coming again. However, they eventually did, and swarmed in good-humoured fashion over our workshops and studios. It all culminated in a farewell supper at which fond speeches were made celebrating the international brotherhood of satire. Tears were shed, and many toasts were drunk, and it was all unbelievably amiable, until we hit on the idea of a jokes competition.

The Russians' head comic writer kicked off with a long, almost impenetrable story about a miserable family of worms living in a dung heap, the culmination of which appeared to be that they thought happiness could be achieved by moving – to the dung heap over the road.

Polite laughter. But our British champion comic writer obviously felt something a shade more punchy would elicit a better response. 'What,' he asked, 'is the difference between your mother and a terrorist?' No one knew, so he naturally supplied the answer: 'You can negotiate with a terrorist.'

There was shocked Slavic silence, until the largest and most aggressive Russian menacingly demanded to know, 'What do you mean – my mother?'

At this point our jokesmith tried to extricate himself by explaining that no slur was intended on any specific Russian mother – the gag only applied to the idea of motherhood in the most general sense, anybody's mother, even his own personal mother who, of course, he held in the very highest esteem.

'Ah,' said the Russian, suddenly drained of belligerence, 'you mean *your* mother. Ho, ho, ho.'

With this interpretation it became possible for us all to raise our glasses to 'the British joke'. Despite these festivities, or maybe because of them, I was beginning to feel that the Russians were more interested in travelling towards a satirical show than actually arriving. So I was very agreeably surprised a few months later when I received a fax from Moscow with the news that *Rubber Souls* had devised a New Year's Eve special destined to go out to all the republics. Sadly, I, and possibly they, had underestimated what they were up against. On the night of the broadcast the Russian team were told by their TV controller that it was not a good time to laugh at Boris Yeltsin. The New Year's Eve special remained on the shelf. Subsequently the independent NTV channel did broadcast a version of the show called *Kukli* (*Puppets*) which flourished briefly until Russia's Prosecutor-General launched a criminal action against the makers of the programme for 'publicly humiliating the honour and dignity' of the country's leaders. An NTV executive was quoted as saying plaintively, 'We actually broadcast some *Spitting Image* programmes earlier this year to show how critical the puppets can be, but at the Kremlin I don't think they understood the joke.'

The United States was the one area of the planet that we did actively try to colonize, with only partial success. During the Reagan years we managed to sell three full-length, custom-built shows there, and we also for a while delivered a series of 'shorts' to the CBS network. However, we never did achieve our main ambition, which was to produce a fully fledged series specifically for the North American market.

My disappointment in not realizing this ambition was to a

large extent mitigated by the good time I had in failing. This was entirely due to the companionship of Tony Fantozzi, our American agent, and his mastery of the laconic one-liner. On emerging with him from a TV network headquarters in Los Angeles where I'd obviously failed to make a sale I asked, 'Where did I go wrong?'

'What do you see behind you, Roger?'

'A big building.'

'And next to it?'

'An even bigger building.'

'Yeah. And it's full of lawyers.'

Fantozzi worked hard on the business of improving my sales pitch with the industry's big-wigs: 'Whatever you do, Roger, don't tell 'em that you carve the fucking puppets.' And, being of Italian descent, he was adept at steering me clear of dubious connections: 'Always best to avoid, Roger, people who can have you whacked in the car park.' These pearls of wisdom were delivered from a considerable height by a man who looked rather like Groucho Marx, only with a taste for even bigger cigars.

Fantozzi was the only non-Jewish director of the William Morris agency, although he was inclined to believe that he was descended from one of the lost tribes of Israel that took a left at Naples. At that time the William Morris agency had David Frost and Barry Humphries on its books, along with a host of American stars. Through the agency we were able to secure the services of Frost as a 'presenter' of our American shows to explain our allegedly weird humour to the natives.

On one memorable occasion Fantozzi came to London to inspect the puppets at closer range. He wore gear he deemed appropriate to foreign travel: a safari jacket, a solar topi and an

Tony Fantozzi

extra-large cigar. Thus attired, he rushed me, still in my grubby workshop clothes, to catch the Birmingham train for a fast visit to the puppet studio. 'Good morning, Sir,' said the ticket inspector to Fantozzi, with exaggerated respect. 'Taking him out for the day, are we?' A delighted Fantozzi told me, 'I just love the humour around here.'

Aside from British humour, Fantozzi was also keen on singers, a sensible bias as he was married to the singer Patty Clark – 'a big star when I met her'. Latterly Patty has returned to the boards singing in exotic locations like the Coconut Grove in Florida, with Fantozzi in close attendance as her agent. 'This way,' he explained, 'I get to carry the costumes *and* sleep with the star.'

Fantozzi's contacts ranged wide throughout every aspect of the business. It was through him that I met Bernie Brillstein, the legendary agent and manager who helped oversee the careers of John Belushi, Jim Henson of the *Muppets*, Dan Aykroyd and numerous others, at whose feet I was happy to sit. Brillstein recalled being inspired at an early stage in his career when he was approached by the producers of a Broadway musical looking for a Yiddish-speaking actress. 'The only one I knew was Jenny Goldstein. They offered to pay her $500 dollars a week. I said that Miss Goldstein was a star and worth $750 a week. They agreed. So I called her to tell her the news. Guess what? She'd been dead for several years. A raise of $250 a week for a dead performer – I knew this was the right business for me.'

I seized my opportunity and asked Mr Brillstein, 'How come I've been in this business for ten years with what's regarded as a very successful show, but without making any serious money?'

Brillstein answered as follows: 'This is how you make money,

Roger. Foist, you raise all the money for the programme. You put it all in the bank. Then you take a liddle bit out of the bank.' At this point he pinched his thumb and index finger close together to indicate just how 'liddle', before resuming, 'And then you make the programme.'

I knew it was advice I was constitutionally incapable of following, but it was nice to get some insight into the higher wisdom. It did seem to me that American television was an absolute paradise for deal-makers, but perhaps not so beneficial for people wanting to develop original programmes – and, of course, British television would evolve on similar lines through the 1990s.

In the end, I think the reason we never conquered America was not so much because we were too obnoxious, but because we were too costly. The few shows we did manage to get on air were very popular, but not, as Fantozzi pointed out, ratings-wise in the same league as *The Simpsons* which, even with celebrity guest trimmings, could be bought in for the same price, or even less.

One day I asked Fantozzi how he got into show business. He said it was really quite simple. While on military service in Korea he had been successful in ensuring a supply of whisky for the top brass. This had led to his being entrusted with the task of helping to assemble a team of top American pilots prepared to 'nuke' several of the main cities in China. Subsequently, when the war fever subsided, he assisted in the business of quietly dissolving the team with adequate cover stories. Thereafter, he said, he was deemed trustworthy enough to take some responsibility for providing entertainment for American troops in the Far East. So he brought over Pearl Bailey, and never looked back.

CHAPTER TWELVE

TRASH FOR CASH

For those of you who have heard the story about how Steven Nallon and I were discovered in compromising circumstances in a Birmingham hotel room, I would just like to sketch in a few extra background details. Steve and I were in Birmingham on a highly responsible business mission, promoting the *Spitting Image* Mrs Thatcher book for the benefit of a conference of sales representatives. We were both very properly dressed for the occasion.

I, for once, was wearing a suit; Steven, our distinguished Mrs Thatcher 'voice' on the TV show, was fully kitted out and coiffed as Mrs Thatcher. The sales reps were most appreciative of how we looked and what we had to say. After our presentation we retired to the hotel room assigned to us by the conference

Nallon and Law

organizer so that we could change into more workaday attire – me, out of the suit into something sloppy; Steve, out of his Mrs Thatcher attire into man's clothing.

This twin operation, conducted on the side of the bed, had just got to the point of me unzipping my fly and Steven's pulling the Mrs Thatcher camisole over his head, revealing the Mrs Thatcher knickers beneath, when the chambermaid walked in, emitted a piercing shriek, and fled.

It does, I think, go to show that there is sometimes less in these situations than meets the naked eye. Many years later when the tabloid press was salivating over a two-in-a-bed story allegedly involving the Prince of Wales and a palace servant, I was among the first to perceive, based on previous experience, that there was most probably a perfectly innocent explanation.

However, it might properly be argued that the director of a major entertainment company should always be on guard against anything that might compromise his, or his company's, dignity. On the other hand, conventional wisdom rarely applied to *Spitting Image*. Indeed, in the interests of the company there were few indignities to which we would not ultimately stoop.

Just as there is said to be no business like show business, there was no show business quite like *Spitting Image* business. By the late 1980s we were turning over a colossal £5 million a year, and still managing to get ourselves in deep trouble. There was even a suggestion that we were on the verge of trading fraudulently, i.e. without sufficient assets to cover our rising indebtedness. I tried to comfort Peter Fluck with the thought that if we were ever sent to jail for illegal trading none of the other inmates would be at all interested in our wrinkly old bottoms. But he was a hard man to console.

The central business problem for *Spitting Image* was that it was exceptionally labour-intensive for twenty-four weeks of the year, when a series was running or in pre-production. But we could not just let a uniquely skilled staff go during the other weeks. They had to be on the payroll, or long-term contracts, for us to have any hope of keeping them together for the next series. So in the off series weeks we literally had to make work to keep their interest alive and of course help pay their wages. Hence the importance of the Mrs Thatcher book and assorted other merchandising operations, some of which were profitable, some decidedly not. The problem of relating activity to profitability was by no means confined to the foot-soldiers in the enterprise. It went right to the top.

If the company was ever in danger of making money Peter and I could be relied upon to come up with some lunacy that squandered thousands faster than Barbara Amiel in a fashion house. Bored with puppets, Peter devised an animatronic Ronald Reagan sporting an uncontrollable and extendable erection. It really was a genuine pinnacle of invention, years before Viagra, but not strictly commercial, even for the likes of us. More practically, Peter also tried to extend the benefits of puppet technology to human limb-fitting mechanisms – a thoroughly worthy research enterprise, but again not strictly in our line of business.

On one occasion Peter and I managed to flag down the great management guru, John Harvey-Jones, when he was visiting Limehouse Studios. Very kindly he consented to make a tour of our workshop and conduct a cursory examination of our books. 'What you have here,' he said, by way of a verdict, 'is not a business, it's a hobby.'

The problems were compounded by the fact that a staff recruited for qualities of inventiveness and irreverence, as well as skill, is not by its nature expert at taking orders. When the disorderly world of *Spitting Image* first came into contact with the smooth running of Central's Birmingham Studios, the Studio Controller said of the new arrivals, 'We need some of them in every society, but perhaps not a lot.' In practice, this meant that projects that engaged the staff's imagination, like the Thatcher book, the chicken song or the design of rubbery dog chews ('Throw a politician to your dog'), could excite high levels of industry. Indeed on some projects the staff had to be deterred from overworking. One such was our *Rubber Johnnies Book*, which could also function as a bellows: as the reader turned the pages, up popped inflated condoms in the shape of world leaders. But motivation could falter, or even die, on less fascinating business assignments. Not that anyone was ever idle. Rather like I had been on the *Sunday Times*, people always found interesting stuff of their own to do if the company's work got slack or was not sufficiently congenial. Unlike the *Sunday Times*, however, there was no mega-millionaire at the back of *Spitting Image* ready to bail the operation out in times of crisis. For us, even with a top ratings TV show still commanding an audience of over 6 million, bankruptcy loomed.

In an effort to balance the books, if nothing else, outside experts were called in, all of whom sang a similar refrain: too much over-manning and too little coordination of staff effort. The consequence of these dysfunctions was said to be: too much pursuit of fancy, money-wasting notions, while actual money-making opportunities, particularly in areas like advertising, were being ignored as too boring. As these insights were being drip-fed into our system, a motley crew of entrepreneurs could be observed in the waiting room outside discreetly inquiring about our health. Fortunately, it was bad enough for them to lose interest. Meanwhile three of the show's original five founders – Tony Hendra, John Lloyd and Jon Blair – had moved out of the puppet business altogether.

From this Weimar-like state of confusion and uncertainty, a Fuhrer inevitably emerged. In March 1991 I formally became chairman of Spitting Image Productions with a majority share-holding in the enterprise. I did not seek this high office; on the other hand I did not avoid it. Richard Bennett, whom we had recently taken on as financial director mainly because he was the first accountant I could actually understand, had told me that the days of the chiefs all scampering around like Indian braves simply had to end. There had to be just one chief, actu-ally acting like a chief, and as Peter Fluck had no appetite for the role it had to be me.

I could hear my father cackling in his grave. After a lifetime spent evading serious responsibility, here I was, aged 50, ulti-mately sharing his terrestrial destiny as a kick-ass capitalist try-ing to impose his will on the unruly. Fortunately, our problem was writ large. We had almost £2 million in debt to clear, and the near certainty that the TV show, already losing some of its spark, would soon be pulled. In fact, it would linger on until 1996 when I was not entirely unhappy to see it go. It was clear to me, as it was to Central TV, that its day was done. Besides which, the show's demise brought an end to the long 'make work' intervals, making it much easier to humanely adjust staffing to more realistic levels.

To clear the debt I instituted what became known as the 'trash for cash' policy which, simply stated, was that no enter-prise was too demeaning if it carried with it the certainty of a fat profit. Those who could not stomach the policy left (which was part of its point), while those who stayed tended to work with more company focus, on account of knowing that their wages depended on it. The overall objective for me and my two watchful business lieutenants, Richard Bennett and Joanna Beresford, our managing director, was our survival as a viable independent production company, with or without the TV show.

In pursuit of trash for cash we waded deep into the advertising market, soliciting work all round the planet. We did bouncy dancing puppets for Sakuraya Stores in Japan; commercials featuring a chicken as a male stripper among many strange offerings for the German market; a loquacious canine character for an agency in New York; assorted talking crocodiles, exploding cattle – you name it, we did it. On the home front, we blazed (almost literally) an advertising trail with the 'I Can't Believe It's Not Butter' commercials with our puppet cows doing many excellent things like abseiling, playing the banjo, cooking fried eggs and firing Uzi submachine guns. Small wonder that Pedigree Chum and Cadbury's Cream Eggs also joined the queue for our services.

Though deeply transitory, these enterprises were not unchallenging. We had particular difficulty with a retake of the frog and the prince situation required by a German client. A wonderfully handsome actor had been recruited to address his girlfriend, who had been unfortunate enough to scratch a spot which transformed her into an animatronic frog. But try as we might we could not get the actor to deliver his lines correctly. Ingenuity saved the day when we got the frog to take on the speaking part instead.

A French advertising agency commissioned three human-sized tuna fish for a job in Paris. The fish had to be capable of dancing and singing and rolling their eyes. So we piled over to

Paris with the flexible fish and their puppeteers, and found the city in the grip of a heat wave. The shoot really defies description, with the puppeteers having to be filleted out of the fish every fifteen minutes and checked for vital signs. The French technicians rather enjoyed this as Louise Gold, our Amazonian lead puppeteer, would emerge steaming, looking like the well-endowed winner of a wet T-shirt competition. But what with the unbearable heat, the language difficulties and the general chaos, I was beginning to crack, apparently noticeably. The day was saved by our workshop manager, Andrew Robey, drawing me to one side and saying, 'Look, Roge, why don't you just sit down? The boss crying is bad for morale.' Once I'd been sidelined the youngsters were able to finish the job.

However, I did find the advertising work quite intriguing. In the days when Luck and Flaw were vainly trying to sell out to the advertising world, we came to feel that caricature and advertising had to be essentially antipathetic – the former being largely negative in conception (i.e. against something or somebody), while the latter had to be positive. Looking back I realize that our mistake was to assume that advertising had to be about stunting up utterly amazing special effects of the chameleon meets rainbow variety. What we should have been doing was looking for a way of fusing the negative and the positive together with the comparatively simple device known as humour.

For all its challenge, and occasional fun, nobody would seriously want to devote a career to devising the kind of stuff we were coming up with. In company terms, though, our advertising blitz did its job, as we hauled ourselves back into the black. And we had a large stroke of luck that enabled us to keep our more genuinely creative juices going, making a television movie of *Peter and the Wolf*, Sergei Prokofiev's classic children's story.

The idea had originated with Claudio Abbado, the Italian maestro, saying to Christopher Swann, a producer of classical music programmes, that he thought Prokofiev's fantasy would work very well with *Spitting Image* puppets. We warmed to the idea, but when we worked out the cost we estimated it coming in at around £650,000 – about three times the cost of an average *Spitting Image* show. It was expensive because all the puppets could only be used once, unlike those on the show which, with running repairs, could be used again and again. And they had to be of much higher quality, partly because they needed to be on screen much longer, and partly because we conceived the story as needing a number of live action sequences which required the puppets to vie for attention with real actors.

As we had no risk capital of our own to put into the enterprise it was decided that we should try to go the co-production route. A joint company, Spitting Swanns, was formed with a specific mandate to raise funds for the project overseas. And pledges of money did indeed come in from a number of sources in Europe, including a major German recording company. But not alas quite enough. Then Richard Bennett rang me one day with tremendous news of a key contribution that had just been made by the Chancellor of the Exchequer, Norman Lamont. His Black Thursday had, at a stroke, raised the value of the foreign funds committed to us by some 20 per cent without our having to raise another deutschmark, lira or franc. We were suddenly in business.

It would be wrong to imply that I knew absolutely nothing about classical music, though the only *Carmen* I was aware of had the surname 'Miranda' and a lot of fruit on her head. Abbado, however, seemed ready to overlook the limits of my musical education, as long as I did not take too many liberties with the story line of a boy in a forest, on intimate terms with a duck and bird, who has a serious altercation with a wolf.

Some liberties were taken, not all of them initiated by *Spitting Image*. It was the responsible classical music lover, Christopher Swann, who had the brilliant idea of a duck with a serious drink problem. This allowed us to feature a marvellous Esther Williams-type underwater sequence of the duck surging down to locate the bottle of vodka he had dropped in the pond. Even so, the business of creating a credible drunken duck created severe technical problems. Eventually we wound up with seven duck bodies which could, when necessary, be interlocked with the one duck head, which we called 'the hero head'. The simplest body construction was just an ass on a stick to represent him as he prepared to plunge down for his vodka, but the ones for the other duck locations – underwater, waddling on land and lurking inside the wolf's stomach – all had to be perfectly formed.

My relations with Abbado, who had Communist credentials aside from being a friend since schooldays of one of my favourite playwrights, the anarchist Dario Fo, were extremely cordial, but not issue-free. We both felt that the story should have some politics in it, if only to acknowledge the fact that while Prokofiev was writing and composing *Peter and the Wolf* back in Moscow in 1936, Stalin was down the road in the Kremlin working on his Great Purges. My idea was to have the three incompetent huntsmen in the story played by puppets of Lenin, Stalin and Trotsky, but for some obscure ideological reason Abbado would not have Trotsky. Finding ourselves unable to agree a correct party line, we compromised by having them played by puppets of the Marx Brothers – Groucho, Chico and

Harpo. Stalin would feature, but he had only a very tiny role, as a couple of broken busts inside the wolf's digestive tract.

There were also problems of political correctness of a slightly different order. It became clear that the puppeteer required to manoeuvre inside the frighteningly heavy wolf rig was well beyond concealment on camera. My proposal was that we should train up somebody with no legs to do the job. This ran into serious opposition on the grounds that it would undermine the puppeteer's art as well being exploitative of the disabled. So I got a very fit young man with no legs who did an absolutely wonderful job inside the wolf costume, and later said that his experience during the days on the set had been among the best in his life. Vindication seemingly was mine, though there were still some question marks over my sensitivity in these areas.

For the final scene in our story, which we set in a circus, I needed an extra supply of live actors to mingle with the puppets. My aim was to achieve a Fellini-like effect, exhibiting huge disparities between the characters. I therefore rang a famous theatrical agency to ask if they could furnish me with a very tall man who was confident on stilts and some dwarfs. I thought the phone had gone dead. Then a very precise voice came back, 'We don't do dwarfs, Mr Law, but we do have some extremely short people.'

The end-product, directed by Christopher Swann, Steve Bendelack, *Spitting Image*'s most seasoned director, and myself, with the real Roy Hudd playing Prokofiev, narration provided by Sting, live action performed by the Théâtre de Complicité, and with Claudio Abbado fronting the Chamber Orchestra of Europe, was first broadcast on BBC 2 on Boxing Day 1993, where it did commendably well against ITV's main offering of the evening – *The Spitting Image Panto*.

171

Some months later, after it had been screened in several other countries, *Peter and the Wolf* won an International Emmy. I was not normally too enthralled by such awards, which rained down like confetti in the high days of *Spitting Image*, but in this instance, after so much 'trash for cash', it was very agreeable to have some outside confirmation of merit.

The other less publicly celebrated personal triumph of this period was my decision to pay attention to my doctor, who pronounced me a prime candidate for cirrhosis of the liver if I did not stop drinking. As I had always regarded heavy drinking as the most natural companion to heavy work, giving up was not that easy, though a wilful excess of swimming in the Ironmonger Row Baths helped a lot, as did the improvement in my appearance as I trimmed down to a svelte 17 stones.

In the wake of *Peter and the Wolf* we also took the opportunity to 'downsize' the company into new premises, moving away from Docklands into a vacant five-storey building in Nile Street, Islington. With the blessing of our financial guru, Richard Bennett, I used our refreshed liquidity to buy the building. This was not much appreciated by the 'creatives' in the outfit, who saw it as good seed capital for productions going to waste, but life had taught me a keen appreciation for low overhead costs. Inside the new streamlined operation there was some debate about whether we should concentrate solely on animation projects or move into live action comedy productions. In the end we did a bit of both.

My puppet hopes for the future were pinned largely on a character called 'Mr Big', a corporate monster with huge destructive tendencies whom we believed would appeal to children of all ages, especially with words supplied by two lively young writers, Kevin Cecil and Andrew Riley. For a while the

BBC seemed to be of a similar mind, but then changed it. Richard Bennett, making his début as a producer, had more success with *Crapston Villas*, a truly weird stop-motion soap devised and made by Sarah Ann Kennedy. This had a decent run on Channel Four, albeit without setting the Thames on fire. Bennett, though, still cherishes the letter he received from the show's commissioning editor, carefully advising on script content. 'Dear Richard,' it began. 'Further to our phone conversation, I'd like to confirm that our lawyers felt 1) cunnilingus and the like probably OK as long as funny, 2) drug story-lines probably OK as long as there's a pay-off in which retribution occurs (OK in these episodes), 3) but if you could take out the specific reference to E (p. 38, episode 19) it would help, 4) "Jesus Christ" offensive to Christians, but in view of the small number of Christians likely to be watching we compromised on dropping only "Jesus fucking Christ" (p. 23, episode 19).'

Tim Watts and David Stoten, our two brilliant in-house caricaturists, provided a boost to our collective ego in 1995 when their animated film *The Big Story*, produced by Spitting Image, was nominated for an Oscar. But it was becoming clear that the terms of business in the TV world were turning against us. With the big money chasing the bankable stars, shows without stars, which included most of our projects, were getting the full disbenefit of the cutbacks. The era of 'cheap programming' had arrived.

We toyed with the idea of a puppet cooking programme, which I estimated we could bring in at £50,000 a half hour. Bendelack told me to stop wasting my time as cooking shows, with real cooks, were coming in around £10,000. 'They can't be any good,' I commented. 'You're not getting the point, Roger,' said Bendelack. 'At that price they don't *have* to be any good.' Bendelack had sussed long before the rest of us that multiple-choice TV really only multiplies choice between varieties of nothing very much. You could admire the bandwidth, but not expect much in terms of programme thickness. Had *Spitting Image* been invented in the mid-1990s, instead of the early 1980s, it would never have got on air.

Meanwhile the trashy side of things was going almost too well, as our advertising work opened up new avenues of enterprise. We would get calls from major companies asking for assistance with their in-house entertainment for corporate shindigs in some hotel or another. Videos featuring caricature puppets of the boss and other company big-wigs were a popular item. We would make them to order. Well, the money was good, and it must be considered at least one step up from supplying the Strippogram – literally in one case

One highly personal request was made by a woman who wanted a life-size effigy of her rich American husband for his birthday. We made him nude as she had agreed to supply his clothes shortly before the actual date. Eventually the puppet, fully attired, was delivered to the couple's favourite restaurant, and when the birthday boy arrived he found his wife sitting at a table for two with his doppelgänger. It all went swimmingly at the time, but by some oversight the mould for the rich birthday boy somehow got confused with those being used to provide bit part characters for the TV show, with predictable consequences. Our once satisfied customer naturally took umbrage. We were loath to destroy our own creation so it was left to Richard Bennett, our finance director, to track it down and pop the rich American's lookalike into the incinerator and take a club hammer to his mould.

As far as possible we tried to supply the business service to only the most respectable outfits, though the Chicago-based accounting firm, Arthur Anderson, subsequently rather let us down by becoming far too closely entwined with Enron. Merrill Lynch, the international investment company, also sought us out and expressed deep appreciation of the final product. So much so that their man in the London office said we should have charged a lot more for our video.

Some weeks later, I think prompted by a grateful Merrill Lynch, I got a call from a top Republican Party official in New York asking if we could kindly supply a puppet caricature of Bill Clinton smoking pot and, as obviously as possible, inhaling deeply. The man at Merrill Lynch was clearly disappointed when I told him I was obliged to turn down the request on the grounds that partisan politics and satire did not mix. It cost us a good pay day, but it was nice to know that my puppets still had a vestige of integrity left. Some years later I was approached by Al-Jazeera, Bin Laden's favourite TV station, with a request for performing puppets likely to appeal to its audience. Again, they were not even tempted, although I was.

By late 1996 Spitting Image Productions was down to three full-timers – myself, Richard Bennett and a whizz young producer, scarcely out of her teens, called Dolly Course – from a peak payroll of close to 100 at the beginning of the decade. All the other people involved with the company worked on a freelance or short-term contract basis. And we were making more actual profit than the original mammoth enterprise ever did. From time to time Peter Fluck would come languidly by to inspect this miracle of modern management, and to keep me abreast of his own post-puppet researches into chaotic constructions – intricate mobiles which he claimed somehow illuminated the Chaos Theory. It sounded fairly potty to me, but I could not help noticing that he seemed very happy in his work, with the mark of contentment evidenced by the little tum protruding from his once spare frame.

I, on the other hand, with the booze problem licked (as much as it ever can be) had become a lean, mean human machine in keeping with the lean, mean company I was running. You could say I was almost a Thatcherite success story, with the unfortunate rider that I, unlike Peter, was seriously unhappy in my work. By degrees I had managed to construct a life which required me to be a businessman first, and an artist as an increasingly distant and demoralized second. This was not how I came in, nor was it how I wanted to go out.

Over the next year I quietly wound the business down to vanishing point. This was not an exhilarating experience, but there were some magic moments along the way. Part of the process of company dismemberment meant relocating almost 1,000 caricature puppets and their moulds which were no longer welcome in the Nile Street Studios. Eventually, I found the perfect home for them, less than a mile from where Deirdre and I lived in the East End.

In those days Three Mills Island Studios, situated in a sequestered 11-acre site off the Bow Road, were very little known outside the film industry, though they later became internationally celebrated as the location setting for *Big Brother*, along with *Lock, Stock and Two Smoking Barrels*, not to mention Mike Leigh's *Topsy Turvy* and *London's Burning*. The man who achieved this transformation was Edwin Shirley, a truly exotic character. A one-time David Bowie and Rolling Stones roadie, Shirley went on to create the Edwin Shirley Trucking Company – 'You rock, we roll' – dedicated to getting rock tours from A to Z. In the years that Edwin rolled while his customers rocked one of the key sound systems that got damaged was his ears. Talking business with Edwin always had to be done at full volume, though, happily, his sense of balance remained unimpaired in all important respects. Towards the end of dinner one evening at my place he fell from his chair and barrelled across the room, emerging upright at the end with his glass of wine still in his fist, and still full.

Edwin's vision was to create a Venice of the East End incorporating the three gin mills (once bonded warehouses), the nearby sewage works and the old gasometers smack in the middle of the Lea Valley waterway. And on a good day I could see it too. In the meantime he gave a lot of encouragement to small creative enterprises. For over a year Three Mills provided the premises and Spitting Image a 35 mm camera for *The Periwig Maker*, a stop-motion film that got its two young makers, Annette and Steffen Schaffler, nominated for an Oscar. Providing storage for 1,000 puppet characters was not in the same imaginative category, but Edwin, flexible as ever, was up for it.

Some weeks after the puppets had been bedded down in their new home at Three Mills, I received a call from an academic in Dusseldorf. He told me that his institute was interested in acquiring some of the *Spitting Image* puppets of German leaders. What had we got to offer? I said that from memory I knew we had a Chancellor Kohl in pretty good condition as well as a Willy Brandt, a bit dog-eared but capable of restoration. But I suggested the best policy would be for him to come over and look through the range himself. By the time he arrived in Nile Street I also remembered that we had a particularly fine Adolf Hitler in almost mint condition.

I mentioned the existence of a Hitler puppet to the man from

Dusseldorf, but he did not seem to take it on board. We took a taxi out to the East End together, and as we walked towards the entrance to Three Mills Island Studios I tentatively broached the subject of Hitler again – Was he quite sure about not wanting his puppet? – and inadvertently touched a nerve. The academic then gave me a very stern talking to about modern Germany having absolutely no interest in Hitler whatsoever.

At this point, as if on cue, some twenty film extras dressed as SS men came jackbooting into view, before coming to a fierce halt in front of us and rounding off their performance to camera with a resounding 'Sieg Heil!'

'Yes,' I was able to say to my new German friend, 'nobody's at all interested in Hitler these days.'

CHAPTER THIRTEEN

NOT QUITE DEAD YET

I am lying in bed in the guest wing at Dartington Hall in deepest Devon. The room is neat, clean and suitably monastic for a place that attracts its fair share of primal screamers in its attempt to corner the alternative medicine market. The view outside is equally therapeutic. Beyond the restored medieval hall and courtyard, there are blossom trees and trimmed lawns which give on to a magical landscaped garden. In the middle distance there is a line of yews, known as the Apostles, still as in an etched print. At this hour you can hear the snails snore.

Wandering down through this vision towards Dartington Pottery, a collection of rustic buildings huddled beside the estate's mill stream, where Britain's most famous potter, Bernard Leach, found refuge before the war, I begin to detect signs of life. It is not long past seven o'clock but I can see that Marianne de Trey, who lives in the wooden house that Leach once inhabited, is already busy in her studio. I know that Marianne, now well into her eighties, feels she still has much work to do, combating the rise and rise of mass-produced pottery.

As the day gently unfolds there is strong sense of industry about Dartington Pottery, but not of a driven variety. Unlike the energetic, deadline-chasing chaos of the *Spitting Image* workshop, it operates on a more transcendental plane. Not too much of an extraneous nature happens to deflect the course of quiet, concentrated activity. The big news on this visit was occasioned by Stephen Course, the pottery manager, leaving the hand-brake off in his estate car, and accidentally ram-raiding the throwing-room window.

Through the later years of *Spitting Image*, pottery became my relief and Dartington was my favourite refuge, a place where I could chill out and explore the limitless possibilities,

and improbabilities, of modelling in clay. I never expected to make much money out of this association, and never did, though my very first steps in the craft were entirely motivated by greed.

Back in the early 1980s, before *Spitting Image* loomed into view, Peter Fluck and I tried to haul ourselves out of an economic crisis by making caricature ceramics, of which the Mrs Thatcher teapot is the best-remembered example. Ignorant of production processes, we went to Royal Doulton for guidance, but they, unamused by our prototypes, showed us the door. But there was no stopping us. I went to Stoke and put together our own production team involving a mould-maker, a pottery and a couple of painters – moonlighting from Royal Doulton. Over the ensuing months I became very attached to the Potteries and its quirky people. But while their skill could be breathtaking, some of our dealings with 'Planet Stoke', as Peter called it, bordered on nightmare. As orders for the first caricature mugs came in, boosted by colour magazine coverage, supplies from Stoke trickled to a halt. I hurried up to the crime scene in the Midlands, more Clouseau than Holmes perhaps, but determined to get the root of the problem.

The painter I quizzed blamed the toxic smell of the glaze, the chill factor in the garage where he did his extramural work, and a chronic bad back. 'Whichever way you look at it, Roger, sooner or later I've got to bend down and pick up the mug.' The mould-maker also left me none the wiser about the production moulds glitch, but he did produce one of the most memorable put-downs I have ever experienced. 'Last night,' he said, 'I saw the Aurora Borealis while standing in my back garden. And quite frankly, Roger, I don't need this kind of aggression from you or anybody else.'

Janice Tchalenko

182

I never did manage to locate the precise malfunction on 'Planet Stoke', but my interest in ceramics, born out of cupidity, continued out of love. Some years later when Pablo Bach, fresh out of Argentina, joined us on the *Spitting Image* modelling bench, I found someone else to share my enthusiasm. The high point for both of us came when we started a close collaboration with Janice Tchalenko, an established potter famed for her large stoneware vessels with bold glazes and patterns. Janice not only knew her stuff, but she also knew her way round the esoteric pottery world. She was my introduction to Dartington.

For both Pablo and myself I think part of the appeal of pottery lay in our desire to reclaim control over what we did. Puppet-construction can be fun, but a puppet's appeal depends as much on what is done with it as what it looks like. Besides, it is highly disposable. With ceramics we at least gave ourselves a chance of achieving an end result that was not totally ephemeral. What was in the collaboration for Janice was not so obvious. But she liked the challenge and stimulus of working with artists in other fields, having previously worked on projects with the painter John Hinchcliffe and the sculptor Richard Wentworth. She also liked the idea of our bringing modelling back into mainstream ceramics. And she liked a laugh.

The first public fruit of our association was *Seven Deadly Sins*, exhibited at London's Victoria and Albert Museum in 1993. I designed the exhibition space to resemble a car wash. The entrance was hung with black polythene strips which the visitor pushed through into a dark room where the seven sins were theatrically spot lit at eye level. Some liked it very much. Witness the *Craft Magazine* review: 'Spitting Image's modelling skills combine with Tchalenko's luscious sense of colour and texture to produce a rich body of work which acknowledges, and sits happily within, the ceramic tradition of high decoration.' Some were not so keen. Witness Stephen Woodruff's critique in *Ceramic Review*: 'The pieces are described (in the catalogue) as "curious, surreal and fantastical". Substitute vulgar, crass and crap and you have a more precisely descriptive title for the display (these lumps of rubbish are actually on display at the Victoria and Albert Museum).' It got worse for poor Mr Woodruff. After the show closed, the V& A bought all our 'lumps of rubbish' so they could become part of the permanent display.

Few reviewers could resist making the crack about *Seven Deadly Sins* being our choice of subject-matter because it required no original research on my part. This was calumny. In reality we had some difficulty recalling 'Lust', and we all had to work particularly hard on 'Sloth'.

Janice, Pablo and I got our act together again in 1996 for a more ambitious exhibition called *Modern Antiques* at the Richard Dennis Gallery in Kensington Church Street. By this time the appearance of our work had been much improved as a result of Stephen Course's research at Dartington. When Janice and I first started collaborating on modelled work we found that the decorative technique normally used – coloured oxides on a white glaze – tended to obscure the detail of the modelling and carving. One solution was salt-glazing, but this process restricts the palette because few colours can survive firing in a salt-glaze kiln. Stephen Course's experiments with high-temperature, computer-controlled reduction firing eventually produced the answer. He became aware that some transmutation glazes, as well as having great colour depth without the need for any white glaze underneath, also 'ran off' the modelling, leaving the parts in highest relief thinly covered. The effect showed off the modelling perfectly while still providing

Law and Course, Dartington

the required brilliancy of colour. Backed by expertise of this quality, I tell Janice, we really should be able to get rich making pots. No chance, she says, at least not until we are long dead. In an effort to speed this process I plan to leave several vessels with Stephen Course at Dartington against the day of my death. He will then, acting on prior instruction, glaze them with my cremated bone ash, and the resulting final run will be sold in a London gallery, proceeds to my grandchildren, at an exhibition to be called *A Limited Edition of Roger Law*.

There is one ironic postscript to my ceramic career. The only pieces of mine to achieve significant value were the very first crudely made Mrs Thatcher teapots, which Peter Fluck and I originally retailed at £13.50 a throw. Somehow they managed to become collectable, and when I last checked they were changing hands in the region of £500 to £600.

My other source of relief from *Spitting Image* was a modest line in public speaking. With a couple of puppets in tow I could command reasonable fees on what is known as the lecture circuit in a way that satisfied my mild exhibitionist tendencies, though not much else. I had half thought of making this a steady occupation after *Spitting Image* closed its doors, until I landed 'the big one'. The occasion was a high-powered conference on the theme of Whither Europe at the Baltimore Hotel in Coral Gables, Miami, where the scheduled 'star speaker' was to be John Major, Britain's most recent ex-Prime Minister. The fat cats and politicos invited to the conference had indicated a desire for some light relief after the evening session, and I was to be it.

Before leaving London I routinely packed the Chirac and Blair puppets, in keeping with the European theme. Then I got a call requesting Bill Clinton and Mrs Thatcher – and the

Queen, Cherie Blair and Hillary Clinton just had to come too. Then I heard on the grapevine that John Major had asked the organizers to make sure that his puppet would not put in an appearance. So it became essential to pack him too.

I now had so much luggage that I asked the organizer if I could bring Dolly, our producer, to help keep track of the stuff. This was OK. On the day before we left I glanced at the tickets we had been sent and noticed that Dolly was booked as cargo, listed with the puppets. I rang Miami to explain that Dolly was a person, and the ticket was changed. On arrival in Miami we found that the understanding organizer had adjusted Dolly's original puppet status to become my paramour, booking us into a double room. So I had to ring the organizer again to explain that we were close friends, but not that close.

The Biltmore Hotel is a wonderful 1920s extravaganza in the style of William Randolph Hearst's Xanadu. It boasts more luxury extras than you can shake a stick at, a stretch limo service to and from the airport, and an elegantly appointed 'Al Capone suite'. Dolly thought it all wonderfully 'cool bananas' and was well relaxed, while I, apprehensive before the big gig, fussed over my presentational materials – video tapes, 35 mm slides and my platoon of puppets.

To take my mind off my talk I sat in on John Major's address on economic and monetary union which, to my amazement, I could almost understand. Keeping awake was the main problem, though I did find myself moved by one of Major's characteristically self-deprecating jokes. 'I met a politician in Georgia recently,' he said, 'who told me he had been re-elected unopposed. If I had been unopposed in the British election I would still have lost.'

In the Biltmore banqueting hall that evening, trussed for

maximum effect in my Norfolk tweed suit, I did happen to notice that the sky had gone a very peculiar colour – a virulent deep jade. Minutes before I was due to mount the podium the wind began whipping up to a tornado-like force and the palm trees bent double. Sheet lightning tore across the heavens every few seconds, and the thunder crashed like toppling buildings. The Spanish-style chandeliers above us flared, fizzled, fused and died. Total blackness descended on the Biltmore, and some people began to panic and make for the doors. I was asked if there was something I could do ... anything ... that could divert people's attention from the fact that the world seemed to be coming to an end. With my way illuminated by hand-held torches I tottered up to the podium, clutching the puppet Clinton, with whom I tried to ad lib a few disjointed, off-colour jokes. The hall went on emptying, fast. If anything, faster, though whether the accelerant was provided by the storm or the quality of my performance I cannot say. Strobe-lit by the lightning flashes, I felt like a cross between Dr Frankenstein, holding up his creation, and Richard III on Bosworth Field offering his kingdom for a horse, anything to get the hell out. It was genuinely tragic stuff.

Next day we discovered that Coral Gables had been hit by its worst storm in five years. Millions of dollars' worth of damage had been done and people's homes had been blown away. We had got off lightly. For Dolly, with the weather once more conforming to the description in the travel brochures, everything was again 'cool bananas'. To her the experience was no worse than another bad day at the office. But it had left its mark on me. I really thought that this kind of caper was a lot more trouble than it was worth, tornado or no tornado.

With *Spitting Image* behind me, the only firm engagements in my calendar became the junkets and dinners which people of moderate eminence put on for one another to keep their old reputations remembered and their tums well fed. Most artistic disciplines have their own mini versions of the Oscar ceremonies, which go almost entirely unreported but which have therapeutic value. Basically, they provide occupation and meaning for those of us past the first flush. We get together and devise awards for the younger generation, and of course for ourselves, primarily for still being alive.

I am all in favour of such goings-on. They certainly provide a pleasant adjunct to existence, but they are not a very good substitute for it. Indeed, contemplation of a long vista of such events stretching inexorably to the grave began to make my feet itch furiously. For some time I had entertained the notion that Australia could hold out an interesting destiny for my late

middle age. After I had pondered, and later rejected, the idea of starting a graduate-level course in animation for students at the Royal College of Art, there were no specific job offers of any quality to hold me back. My children, Shem and Sophie, had long since flown the coop, while my life with Deirdre now revolved around our studio flat in Poplar, part of a conversion of what had once been Dr Spratt's Dog Biscuit Factory.

I tried to infect Deirdre with my belief in the potential renewing power of Australia, to no avail. There was no interesting work for her there, as far as she could see, though she could well understand that a man had to do what a man had to do, no matter how incredibly juvenile it might be. For her part, she had the slightly more pressing matter of a solo exhibition of her quilts in Switzerland.

Thus unblessed, but deeply understood, I flew off to Sydney.

CHAPTER FOURTEEN

THE BLUE BEYOND

The Gay Mardi Gras started on the plane to Sydney. After a flight on which the food was served by stewards wearing black mini skirts with diamante trim, there seemed no point in fighting it. On then downtown to witness the blast past of 'dykes on bikes' – a formation of 200 lesbians, all leathered up and gunning their personal machines. Then, more sedately, came the floats and the marchers, freighted with individual messages.

'Sluts 4 Jesus', 'The Exotic Blooms of Fiji' and 'Absolutely Patsys' were among those that caught the eye. My personal favourite was 'Chelsea Bun', a 7-foot giant wearing a baby pink poodle suit with curly white fur at the ankles and wrists. The majority of the marchers were impressively sporty in appearance, none more so than 'Gay and Lesbian Scuba Divers of New South Wales' – all fit as butcher's dogs. The only beer guts on parade belonged to a contingent marching under the banner 'Queer Irish'. Gayness may be good for you, but Guinness does tend to be fattening. The loudest cheer of all was for the mince past of 'Gay and Lesbian Police'. After twenty years of Mardi Gras the local law enforcers, more commonly known as the Sydney Wallopers, had decided to join in.

As an introduction to the culture of another country it had vivacity and charm, but it was not of course the whole story. Australia has its homophobes as well as its homosexuals, its fat as well as thin, lissom people, its nasty cops as well as its nice cuddly ones. Indeed, only a few days after my arrival Bill Leak, the chief cartoonist and caricaturist on *The Australian*, helped me to a more balanced view with a cartoon about a recent shooting in the street. One cop, standing beside a seriously dead citizen, was shown eyeing another cop with a smoking gun, and saying, 'Why didn't you use your mace?' 'I did,' said the gun-toting cop, 'but it didn't kill him.'

Like any other city with 4 million inhabitants, Sydney has its share of problems. But there was one impression I had on arrival that I've never had to revise. In fact, it would grow stronger the longer I stayed and got to know more of its peculiarities. This was a city that really liked itself.

Appearances in this case were not just important, they were supremely important. Among the Sydneysiders I met early on was Alex Mitchell, once a good mate on the *Sunday Times*, but now repatriated as a senior columnist on Sydney's *Sun Herald*. By way of easing me into the local sensitivities, Alex told me that I had no need to fret about my satirical instincts or conceal them in any way. I could let them roam free in any direction:

'no worries', nobody was likely to get seriously upset. But I should take great care 'never to knock the view'.

He illustrated the point with a cautionary tale. Last year, he had been on assignment in Brazil and had written home in his dispatch, almost as an aside, 'I thought Sydney had the greatest harbour in the world until I saw Rio …' Mega huge mistake. 'Mate, the protest mail came in by the sackload. If I'd said I was going to barbecue a live koala on the steps of the Opera House I would not have got one tenth of the outcry.' Alex suggested that if I couldn't think of anything sufficiently laudatory to say about the city's appearance I should take refuge in Gore Vidal's observation to the effect that 'Sydney is the city that San Francisco thinks it is.'

As it happened (meaning no offence to Rio or San Francisco), Sydney already qualified as the most stunning city I had ever seen. After living and working in London's East End for so many years it was as if someone had suddenly turned on the lights. Any lingering doubts I might have had about leaving England evaporated at the sight of the vast glistening harbour with the Opera House in full sail alongside the huge span of the iron bridge.

Hunting for a place to live, initially I thought I might buy. At this point I came to realize that the life's ambition of every Sydneysider was to get a place with a harbour view. Australian newspapers have thick supplements in full colour catering for this obsession. Lavish and skilful photographs are deployed to illustrate the views afforded by the properties for sale. And if the actual view is insufficiently appealing, a potential one will do. The vendor of one house I looked at had constructed a metal tower for would-be buyers to clamber up so they could appreciate the panorama that would be theirs once they'd built

194

another storey on the existing property. Never mind the flooding in the kitchen, just look at that view.

As my search intensified, I became more expert at decoding the estate agent's prose:

'Make living an art form' meant it's for sale in a tower block.

'Urban opportunity' meant I could turn to the next item.

'Sun-drenched rooms with balcony' meant I'd better move fast.

'Panoramic harbour views, absolute waterfront' meant only millionaires need apply.

'A view that will last a lifetime' meant a member of Kerry Packer's family was looking for something a little more roomy.

Buying property in Sydney, however, is no game for a mug fresh on the scene. The majority of houses are sold through auctions at which the owner and his friends can lustily join in the bidding. The whole process can lead to a feeding frenzy that puts the white sharks in the harbour to shame. So I decided to rent.

By this time I had already identified the neighbourhood best suited to my aspirations and needs. A fifteen-minute bus ride from downtown Sydney brings you to the great sweep of surfing beach – Bondi. Bondi is an Aboriginal word meaning the sound of crashing surf, though now it tends to evoke all that is crass and ephemeral. Having suffered all my life in London as an intellectual lightweight, among Bondi's surfers I felt I could pass as Albert Einstein, if they had any idea who he was.

The seafront at Bondi is life without Mum and Dad for the energetic youth of all nations. As Haight Ashbury in San Francisco was to the 1960s generation, so Bondi's Campbell Parade is to the youth of the Millennium. Shop windows, lamp-posts and empty wall spaces are plastered with computer-printed and hand-scrawled small ads announcing anything from a stuffed koala to a clapped-out kombi for sale. Parts of Bondi give a new meaning to the words 'dormitory town'. A shared room could be rented for around $55 (£22) a week, $100 (£40) for a room to yourself. Again there were codes: 'looking for easy-going flatmates' meant late night raves. 'No bills, no bond, no problems' implied a strong likelihood of plenty of the aforementioned.

But Bondi is by no means all beer and barbies. It was originally built as a working-class suburb and play opportunity. A tram service ran direct from the city centre to Bondi Pavilion, and weekends were good clean fun for all the family. Much of this old Bondi is still in evidence. There are many sturdily built apartment blocks of 1920s and 1930s vintage, and three streets back from the esplanade the streets are demurely suburban. It is true that that surf rats dominate the seafront area, but their infestation is essentially seasonal. Come late autumn they move on to warmer climes. With their migration an older, intriguingly polyglot Bondi emerges into the sunlight (Sydney's winters are not unlike English summers only with sun). Bondi's year-round population is a mix of Australian Anglos, Hungarians, Slavs, Greeks, Italians, Chinese and Portuguese, and much of Sydney's media crowd resting between jobs. Shops cater for all these minorities, including the most recent arrivals, South Africans ('Weir hev yew pokked der kar?') and Russians. In winter Bondi's solid Masonic Hall, emblazoned with the words 'Odessa at Bondi', becomes a fulcrum of social activity with a never-ending stream of weddings and bar mitzvahs. Most evenings at dusk you can hear melancholic violin music drifting down the road from the Russian Club.

If you like your cosmopolitanism spiced with the trimmings

of hibiscus and pink parrots, and the opportunity to see the occasional whale nosing shorewards, it is hard to imagine a better location than Bondi during the off season. It is also the time to move in. By some quirk of the law, estate agents are obliged to demand that rented premises are left clear after each tenancy. As a result garage sales are numerous, particularly in May and June as the surfers move on. I was able to furnish my entire small but pleasantly formed two-room Art Deco apartment at minimal cost from street sales – everything from the bed to the coffee cups, with the exception of the fax machine which I found, in full working order, abandoned by the side of the road. And the apartment, yes, it had it ... a sun-drenched balcony with a view.

The novelist D.H. Lawrence described his encounter with Australia as like walking out of the world and entering 'an open door into the blue beyond'. I now knew what he meant, almost literally. A short step away from my front door and I could on most days go swimming in a sea pool built into the rocks. Oftentimes the blue of the pool and the sea and the sky would seem to merge into each other. The sensation was like breast-stroking through a Mark Rothko painting.

To say I felt instantly at home in Sydney would be to understate the case. It was more like finding that I had suddenly lucked into another state of being, though it did occur to me that if I had grown up in this environment I might have reached man's estate with a seriously blunted satirical faculty. In saying this, of course, I'm implying absolutely no criticism of anybody's 'view'. Sydney may not be the most beautiful city in the world (though I rather think it is), but as an enterprise that started out as a punishment, an open prison and dumping ground for unfortunates we Brits could not be bothered to

hang, it is quite incredible. But then, I would discover that the incredible, on this continent, is not that unusual.

I was faintly acquainted with the saltwater crocodile before I went to Australia. One of the advertisements we fashioned at *Spitting Image* featured a model of the beast addressing a would-be tourist with an engaging smile and saying, 'You won't need a return ticket.' But it was not adequate preparation for the reality. I came close to seeing my need for a return ticket expire while collecting rock oysters in the shallows off the north-east coast of Arnhem Land. Suddenly, what seemed like a huge glinty-eyed U-boat surfaced close by me, intent it seemed on extending its food chain in my direction. Fear, happily, gave my feet wings until I made it up the beach, sans oysters but otherwise intact.

In my ignorance I had thought that saltwater crocodiles were on the verge of extinction. But this, I later learned, was a deeply out-of-date notion. They had apparently come very close to being wiped out back in the 1970s, but a ban on hunting the species ensured their revival. One census estimated that there were 70,000 in the Northern Territory, which would have included mine, and many thousands more in Western Australia and Queensland. There have even been suggestions that limited, licensed hunting of saltwater crocodiles should be resumed to keep the numbers down. I noticed in a recent eco-friendly report the suggestion that only crocodiles at least 13 feet long should be killed. I'm not against this, but it did strike me that huntsmen ready to run a tape measure over these creatures before deciding whether it's appropriate to take a shot at them could be extremely hard to find.

I went to Arnhem Land, some 4,000 miles from Sydney to what Australia calls its Top End, on the recommendation of Herb Wharton, the Aboriginal author, who originally befriended me at the Cunnamulla Lizard Race. One of its advantages, he said, was that white men were very thin on the ground. Indeed, you could only go there by invitation of one or other of the Aboriginal communities, which he could arrange. It was to be my first serious long-haul trip outside New South Wales, offering the promise of a place where I could paint with no deadlines, nothing blocking the view, and nothing to interrupt the flow of colour from the landscape through my brush.

The colours were indeed devastating but I found myself, initially at least, more caught up in the cuisine. The Yolngu people, whose guest I was, are highly skilled hunter-gatherers never returning empty-handed from forays into the bush or the sea. Herb Wharton had told me that eating 'beyond the black stump', outside the white man's Australia, could be a gourmet experience, though I had taken this information with a large grain of salt. But fast food Arnhem Land style – i.e. food caught, cleaned and cooked on an open fire the same day – has no equal. Indeed it has to be tasted to be believed. Oysters are fairly standard fare for the Yolngu, as they attach themselves to the aerial roots of the mangroves. All you do is chop off sections of the mangrove roots until you have oysters in sufficient quantity. Throw the roots on the fire, the shells open up and *Voilà!* You have smoked oysters.

Stingray balls require a slightly higher level of culinary skill, but it's worth mastering if you're lucky enough to make it to Arnhem Land. Your stingray is best caught in the season when the bush is carpeted with white lilies. If the inside of its mouth is a pale whitish yellow, that's good. First, turn over your stingray and cut a smiley face. Take out the liver and place it to one side. Boil the meat of the stingray prior to removing the skin and bones. Wash the cooked flesh in sea water, rinse in freshwater. Mix the raw liver thoroughly with the boiled fish (10 per cent of raw liver). Roll into balls. Close your eyes and eat. Two of these can keep Mike Tyson going for a week.

Art in Arnhem Land is not, as is often the case in England, a social extra. It is the basis for everyday life and sacred law, all of which is connected to the land and sea and has been for over 50,000 years. I could not pretend to fathom all the intricacies of the Yolngu philosophy and their elaborate (unwritten) social rules regarding kin. Perhaps this was just as well. There is a sensitivity to too much encroachment.

Axel Poignant, reckoned to be the finest photographer of Australian wildlife, brought Arnhem Land to the attention of his white countrymen almost half a century before my visit. His photographs of Aboriginal dances designed to appease the carnivorous earth and pay homage to the Rainbow Serpent would later provide inspiration for the choreography in a Covent

Garden production of Stravinsky's *Rite of Spring*. Many years later Poignant's widow Roslyn returned to Arnhem Land seeking out the descendants of the dancers to obtain their permission for her to publish an essay about her late husband's visit. Walking home one evening she was asked, 'Are you the lady with our memories?'

Poignant's black and white images are hard to match, and I soon realized that I would need to acquire a much deeper understanding of the country before I could begin to achieve anything artistically worthwhile with its landscape and its people. Its extraordinary creatures, however, ranging from the kangaroo to the possum, were almost instantly accessible. These I began to draw and paint with schoolboy enthusiasm.

In recent years Arnhem Land has drawn attention to itself well beyond the boundaries of Australia through its reputation as a centre of excellence for bark painting. It sells its art products direct to dealers in America, Japan and Europe. This is an area where white faces do get a look in, but only in a supportive role. At Buku-Larrnggay Mulka Art Centre there is a gallery and print shop run by Will Stubbs, a lawyer of European stock married to a beautiful Aboriginal, Merrkiyawuy Ganambarr. He manages the arts centre under the direction of Yolngu elders who have decreed that only locally harvested materials – bark, ochres, Pandanus, hard and soft wood – can be used in the production of art. The only exceptions are the visually strong linocuts made in the print shop.

Will uses a four-wheel drive to bring in the raw materials from the bush, accompanied by a profusion of spear-carrying hunters, hunters' wives and children, hitching a lift. Will confides to me that such trips always caused him some apprehension at the thought of his overloaded vehicle getting stuck in the mud miles from anywhere. Such worries never clouded the Yolngu mind, on account of home always being wherever they happen to be.

On one of the days I went out with them a Yolngu child, upset for some mysterious reason, started bawling his eyes out. I'd been told that Aboriginals never hit their children so I was interested to see how his mother would react. Cuddles and endearments were tried but to no good effect. But as we were passing a small expanse of water, the mother signalled for an emergency stop. She then proceeded to dunk the howling boy's bum in the water with what seemed like a magically calming effect. For a few moments I saw myself as being in a position to upstage Dr Spock with a new book on baby care, but it was not to be. Once the shock had worn off the boy resumed bawling louder than ever, until he fell asleep.

The business side of the enterprise consisted of Baluka, a local sculptor, identifying trees suitable for the art work. Will would then crash though the bush with his chainsaw and do what was required. Too exhausting even to watch. Gathering the yellow ochre was far less taxing. It was simply harvested from open seams in the ground. We also had to keep an eye out for hollow logs, useful for burial purposes or to decorate and sell at the Arts Centre.

At one point I felt the urge to wander off into the bush on my own, but this met with opposition from a Yolngu guide. I was told this was only done in twos. When I pleaded that it was not my intention to go very far on my own, I was told that was all very well but 'How will we know it's you when you come back?'

I wanted to go to Yalangbara, a beach of huge sand dunes, which I had heard had a sacred significance. Will was up for it, but first it was deemed politic to make for the headman's house in nearby Bawaka. We were ushered in through a kitchen literally shimmering with exotic fish and sea creatures. I asked for permission to go to the sacred beach and was told that this would be in order if I painted the view across the bay for the headman whose eyesight appeared to be failing. In reality I was much keener to paint the baby green turtles I could see doing laps in the headman's plastic bucket, but that was not what protocol required. So I came up with a couple of little impressionistic watercolours of the bay. The headman murmured something to the effect that I painted like a white man. But he didn't hold it against me. I got my permission.

Alone in the hot sand dunes the atmosphere was like an open-air cathedral. Yalangbara is indeed a holy place. The two Djang'kawu sisters, after a long voyage, came ashore here and, hidden from sight in the dunes, gave birth to the Yolngu nation. Imagery of this event is the theme of many bark paintings. The Yolngu people have no need to build sacred monuments. Time is not linear to them. The Creation Sisters arrived yesterday, and will do so again today, and tomorrow, and will continue to do so forever.

CHAPTER FIFTEEN

CHANGE OF LiFE

Although I never regarded time spent wobbling towards Bondi beach on a boogie board as wasted, I still needed work of some kind, preferably remote from puppet construction, and some place to do it. I was fortunate enough to find the latter relatively quickly in a nicely appointed, reconditioned prison cell.

Two of Sydney's main art schools are conveniently housed in what are, by Australian standards, ancient buildings – one in a former Victorian mental institution, the other, even older, in what was a custom-built jail. One morning, shortly after my arrival, I took coffee with Merran Esson, a potter who ran the day-to-day activities of the ceramics department at the National Art School in premises that once constituted Darlinghurst jail. Discussion of my aspirations in the southern

CHANGE OF LIFE

hemisphere led Merran to propose what sounded like an interesting form of captivity. A little over an hour later, with the blessing of Bill Samuels, Merran's departmental chief, I was banged up in a cell in Block 24, with the title 'Artist in Residence'.

I had my work space, along with many powerful evocations of Sydney's brutal past. Darlinghurst jail was built in the 1820s to the design specifications of Francis Greenway, a gifted convicted forger. The basic material is hand-carved sandstone. The convicts did the carving and the constructing, and the original pike and chisel marks can still be seen everywhere. The surrounding stone walls were built some 23 feet high. The men's lavatory area, immediately below my personal cell, was where people were hanged in large numbers. Nearby, I would discover, located above a tub of colourful banksias, were the flogging rings (two cast-iron rings attached to the wall just above head height, now painted the same colour as the room). The current library was once the prison chapel. The reception centre once housed the morgue. The main lecture hall had been the women's prison, while the tree-shaded barbecue area where students and staff often gathered to partake of wine and cheese was once the lime pit – unconsecrated ground for the disposal of executed convicts.

For all this, it was a remarkably pleasant place to work, sheltered from but still part of the bustling city that surrounded it. Most Australian artists – from John Olsen to William Dobell – had done some time at the National. However, the troubles on site were not just part of a dim and distant past.

I had unwittingly pitched up at the National when there was a revolution going on. Until 1997 the school had been under the bureaucratic thumb of TAFE (Technical and Further

Education), which was responsible for technical courses throughout Australia. The National's teachers, all working artists, were cheesed off with what they saw as the surreal teaching edicts emanating from TAFE. The final straw had been the introduction of what was called 'competency-based training'. Under the leadership of Geoff Ireland, the Head of Sculpture, the teachers raised the standard of rebellion. To TAFE, naturally, the idea of an independent art college went down like a pork chop in a synagogue. Writs flew around the courts in all directions, while inside the school the scent of pumped adrenalin mixed with frangipani blossom made a heady cocktail.

I'm inclined to think that my modest, unpaid appointment owed something to this frantic atmosphere. The teachers were actively looking for trouble, and it might have seemed a good idea to hoist an extra known troublemaker on board. In any event, I was not about to complain of the absence of red tape in my case.

Geoff Ireland, I found, was a man with the tenacity of a pit bull. I was told that he had once dropped a stone carving weighing several hundredweight on his toes, squashing them flat like a Tom and Jerry cartoon, but the doctors rebuilt his feet to the point where he could put the boot in more efficiently than the best of them. He was also shrewd. Ireland told me later that the best advice he received during the long and bitter battle for freedom was given him by a public relations man: 'Forget the bureaucrats, they promise everything and deliver nothing. Politicians change policies, bureaucrats just implement.' Taking heed of the advice, Ireland alertly changed tack, and effectively outflanked the courtroom battles. With the support of the Sydney art world he approached Bob Carr, Shadow

Premier of New South Wales, who said if elected he would back the renegades and give them independence. Three weeks after becoming Premier, Bob Carr honoured his promise. The school was re-launched by the international art critic Robert Hughes who, in his youth, had also done time at the National. TAFE's court actions continued but the independent college was on its way.

My part in these great events was trivial, but I could only root for the realization of the fantasy of artists running their own art school. It certainly had a bracing impact on energy levels in my areas of interest. I noticed that potters visiting Australia from far and wide hardly had time to shake off the jet lag before Bill Samuels had them strutting their stuff in Block 24. In fact, the whole place had the kind of buzz that I remembered from earlier periods of creative chaos – in the sixties at the pre-Murdoch *Sunday Times* under the editorship of Harry Evans, and in the early eighties during the formative days of *Spitting Image*, before it became a grind. It may be that such periods are not built to last, but I'm convinced it's when the best work gets done.

The National was a great place to paint or pot or just hang out, but it did not pay the rent for my parallel sybaritic existence in Bondi. For that I had to commute ... to Melbourne. After years spent shuttling between London workshops and Birmingham studios for *Spitting Image*, I thought nothing of setting up a Sydney–Melbourne commuting arrangement. On the map it looks like a similar enterprise. But nowhere, except perhaps Siberia and the American Midwest, can do distances quite like Australia. So when I discovered that it took eleven hours by train to cover the ground between Australia's two major cities I realized that my paid working life would become more obtrusive than I had intended.

210

I seem to have an uncanny gift for arriving in cities when a festival is in progress. On my first day in Melbourne the entire place seemed to be covered in banners with the word 'Moomba' on them. The focus of all the action was concentrated on the banks of the Yarra River where there was much music and rowdy jollity. Some people tell me 'Moomba' is Aborigine for 'Have fun', others that it is the ancient formulation for 'Fuck off'. Despite our common language, and my personal background in satire, I was still finding it hard to be sure when an Australian was kidding me.

After the banners had been taken down, I was able to appreciate that Melbourne was an impressive city with many fine houses – a felicitous by-product of the Gold Rush – and loads of leg-room. Somehow its population of around 3.5 million manages to spread itself over an area the size of London. Not as stunning as Sydney of course, but equipped with some terrific bookshops, which also sold good coffee.

In Melbourne my prime economic function was to act as consultant to a production company I nicknamed 'The Lost Boys'. My new mates lived communally in a pleasant suburban house, *sans* Wendy and Tinkerbell but with a compensating exuberance. Most of them were between relationships – all boys together. On working visits I would take up residence in the garden studio.

It was puppets again, I'm afraid, but I was dimly coming to the realization that maybe I could not have everything. Also I found the work, which mainly consisted of chaperoning a sci-fi puppet TV show, surprisingly enjoyable. This was partly because it was refreshing to be working again with a high-spirited workshop which was up for anything. Aside from puppets we fashioned a large mechanical figure to grace a supermarket

forecourt, and subsequently constructed a gigantic model of the inside of Moby Dick for some reason that I cannot now recall. But the main reason for enjoying it all was the fact the I was not ultimately responsible. The buck stopped somewhere else.

The puppet show also opened another door that was both reasonably profitable and enormously enhancing to my self-esteem. RMIT, the big Melbourne university, decided to engage me for one day a week to teach scriptwriting. It might be thought that my knowledge of scriptwriting would have diffi-culty covering the back of a postage stamp but I inevitably discovered some of its rudiments through having to produce storyboards for cartoon sequences, first in Oregon and more frequently later in the last stages of *Spitting Image*. Anyway, this slim experience enabled me to play the pedagogue, and stay marginally ahead of the wiseacres in the class.

One of the more attractive things I was finding out about Australia was that, while it nurtured an all-round competence, it did not expect people to specialize overmuch. It just does not have a large enough population to support the kind of tunnel-vision expertise that is so much prized in Britain. Bill Samuels, my mentor and protector at the National, aside from teaching, administering and making art, also had a pilot's licence and con-structed his own house from the foundations up. And he was not that exceptional. Among 'The Lost Boys' there was a versa-tile young guy called Hughie, who was very good at puppet con-struction as well as operating them as a puppeteer. One evening I went to a lively Mexican opera at the town hall and there was Hughie again, playing a deft accordion. Next day part of the Art Deco ceiling in my lodgings decanted onto my bed. That evening I came back in time to see the workman putting the finishing touches to its restoration. Naturally, it was Hughie.

I never met an Aussie potter who had not fashioned his own house, studio and kiln. Ask an Australian potter a technical question on any aspect of modelling, glazing or firing and you stand a good chance of getting a helpful answer. This comes from having to do everything for themselves.

Back in Sydney, where I still spent over half the week, I was floundering precisely because I did not have this all-round nous. Even though I had modelled in clay for years there were huge gaps in my knowledge of the craft. My first gas-firing exercise over-fired and literally reduced three weeks of industrious modelling to a heap of coke. This disaster, coupled with my obvious fear of the gas kiln, which I refused to approach without a more practical person in tow, was the cause of much hilarity among others in the department.

At one point I took a detour from modelling into drawing on the pots and glazing them thickly with feldspar. It fell off. One of the tutors tipped me off about the adhesive possibilities of PVA wood glue, bentonite and a food processor. I tried his recipe. It fell off again. Bill Samuels kindly took pity on me, pointing out that the photograph in a pottery book which originally inspired my efforts was probably the best result the maker had achieved in a life spent glazing with thick feldspar. He also said, I think by way of encouragement, 'Failures are a good way to learn and occasionally some "failures" are better than the original.'

Under the impetus of my failures, my classification at the college was shrewdly changed from 'Artist in Residence' to 'Student in Residence' or, as one of the other students elegantly put it, 'Dosser-in-Residence'. I then began to learn a lot of basic stuff about clay and glazes and the eccentric personalities of the kilns from both students and staff. But I never did catch up with the rest of the class. My residency was extended from six months to the full year, so I suppose I must have contributed something, but it certainly was not my ability to fire a kiln.

One happy consequence of my demoted status was my qualification to carry a student card, which chopped a couple of dollars off the price of a cinema seat and entitled me to subsidized travel all round the city. It also gave me access to cut-rate bushwhacking weekends, organized by the students' union, which I took to with great relish, though I again experienced language difficulties.

When they said, 'Bring warm clothes, it will be cold,' it never was. 'This walk is easy for the moderately fit' must have been fashioned with Daley Thompson in mind. Seven hours striding around the Jamieson Gorge in the Blue Mountains just outside Sydney is not easy by any definition. It was exhausting, and it was only the spectacular visuals that kept me going. Plus the lyrebirds. They are incredible mimics. In the Jamieson Gorge they have adopted the roar of the chainsaw as a calling song. The chainsaw has been banned from this national park for twenty years, so knowledge of the sound must have been passed down through the generations from parent to chick. The lyrebird also does a very good line in car alarm imitations, all very exotic and surreal.

My love affair with Australia's strange creatures intensified when I took a trip out to the Healesville Wildlife Sanctuary, a two-hour drive from Melbourne. The platypus keeper let me fondle Corrina, one of his charges. The platypus is a charming and unlikely mammal which seems to make no sense at all until you see it darting and turning at speed under water. Its fur is so thick that it never seems to get wet. The keeper told me that the female platypus has to lead a regular life in the same stretch of

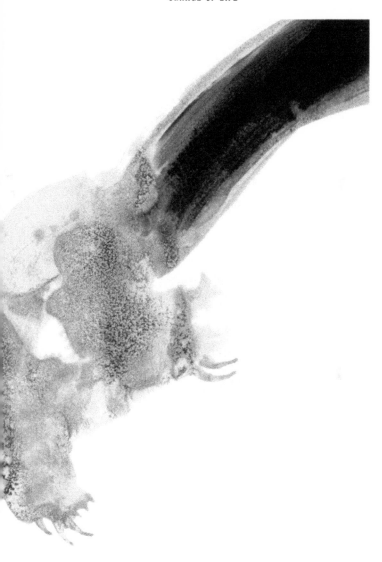

water for seven years before she becomes sexually mature. If all goes well, apparently, she remains on heat for a full seven minutes. The male, meanwhile, is up for procreation for four months in any given year, but if he happens to nod off at the time the female is ready he can blow his chances altogether. In the female's eighth year the male's prospects improve very slightly. He has fifty minutes in which to get his leg over, so to speak. This probably explains why the only platypus born in captivity was at Healesville in 1941 – until 1999 when a second was triumphantly ushered into the world at the sanctuary by Corrina. To be honest, I'm not sure if I have got all the intricacies of the love life of the platypus exactly right, but as my friend the Australian journalist Murray Sayle says, 'Some stories are too good to check.' Drawing these extraordinary creatures gave me a special pleasure. I could hardly wait to get them back to my cell/studio and get them on to plates – platypus plates.

Another great outing was to the potters' jamboree, organized by Janet Mansfield, the delightful and energetic publisher of *Art and Perception* (the potters' bible). It was held at Gulgong, a pretty and historic gold-mining town in New South Wales. The National Art School's ceramic students were invited along. We all lived in tents, and built the largest kiln in the world. The lectures, given by international ceramic superstars, took place in Gulgong's Prince of Wales Opera House, the décor unchanged since the turn of the century, wonderfully run down, chandeliers askew. I kept expecting to turn a corner and catch sight of Edward VII groping Dame Nellie Melba. The stars at night made the sky almost white. The potters' campfires roared away all night and all day. I was shocked to realize that all potters are pyromaniacs.

My more extended trip to Cunnamulla and Eulo for the World Lizard Race Championship in Queensland where I backed the wrong lizard and met Herb Wharton was in a different order of style. Bill Samuels flew me in and out in a Cherokee Lance light aeroplane. Well, I could hardly be expected to slum it as a student every day of the week.

Travel around Australia became my new addiction. You do not have to stray very far from Melbourne or Sydney to get the

feeling of being in a place where the landscape is still very much in charge, and that human beings are pretty much on the same shaky par as other species, tolerated by the terrain but only just. Australia has grandeur, something we don't do in England, and I knew I was going to miss this more than anything when some unfinished business called me home. But I also knew I would soon be back for more. I just loved it. Australia is said to be a young country, but it also happens to be the best place in the world to have the male menopause.

I needed to get back to London to fulfil a commitment I had entered into much earlier to make a film about pottery, but I also had a more personal self-promotion in mind. After fifteen months in Australia I had assembled a fair-sized body of work – over 100 pieces, in fact, comprising prints, watercolours, ceramics and small bronze figures. More than enough for an exhibition, if I could persuade somebody to mount it. There was, however, something of an image problem about the collection: none of the pieces could be classed as caricature or even mildly satirical. I hoped that people could see some wit in my images of the kangaroo, the platypus, the turtle and related species, but they were rendered to be appreciated, and enjoyed, not laughed at. The art market, in common with most markets, likes to operate with the guidance of familiar categories, feeling most confident when it is selling the kind of stuff that has sold before. But there seemed to be no known category for a specialist puppetmaker-turned-animal-life-celebrator.

So it was no wonder that I met with some puzzled responses as I went, portfolio in hand, round the various London dealers and art galleries. People were kind enough about the work, but brows furrowed at the problem of how to place or promote it.

In Agnew's, the super-smart West End dealers, I was pleasantly, but negatively, entertained by an immaculately dressed gentleman. In exasperation at not getting my way, I asked rather aggressively what did he think his gallery was all about. 'Money, dear boy, money,' he said sweetly. He then showed me round the viewing room pointing at each large canvas in turn, saying, '£8,000, £10,000, £12,000.' He did not have to go on for too long. I could tell he was a man with overheads of the kind I had once known so well, and that there was no way my space-hungry, modestly priced stuff could even begin to solve it. We parted on good terms.

My exhibition called *Aussie Stuff: Way Beyond the Black Stump* was eventually put on at the Rebecca Hossack Gallery in Windmill Street, just off the Tottenham Court Road. Rebecca's day job was cultural attaché to the Australian Embassy in London, where she was a kind of Les Patterson figure only a lot better looking. It was said of Rebecca that she was the person mainly responsible for rendering obsolete the joke about the difference between an Australian and a pot of yoghurt (answer, for those still unaware: the yoghurt has a living culture). She made a very nice job of setting up my show, which ran from October through November in the year 2000 and did encouraging, but less than sensational, business.

Pot Shots, the film I conceived, wrote and directed in response to promptings from what might be called the ceramics establishment, took all of one day to get in the can. We shot it with hand-held cameras in tight focus on our star, the energetic man-mountain, Johnny Vegas, a dedicated potter as well as being a brilliant stand-up comedian. For the final editeddown seventeen-minute film I managed to get the illustrious David Attenborough, whose wife was a potter, to do an expert

Johnny Vegas

voice-over. The plot was not too hard to follow. Vegas was required to play a series of unappreciated, near demented historical potters from George Ohr, the 'Mad Potter of Biloxi' down to the present day. He was encouraged to rant against the obtuseness of clay, and bitch generally against the utter injustice of a world that accorded such low status to the potter. For

222

the final sequence I had managed to assemble £60,000 worth of the best British pots, donated to the enterprise by their creators on the firm understanding that they would not survive. These Vegas reduced to rubble in one last huge paroxysm of rage. At the film's British première, screened in the Victoria and Albert Museum, I was happy to observe the potters in the audience exhibiting delight at this wanton orgy of destruction, while their dealers went chalk white.

In its review of the film, the *Guardian* commented that it was 'beautifully shot' and 'instructive', which made pretty heady reading for the boy who had so recently been the dunce of the ceramics class at Sydney's National School of Art. It also said, somewhat more cryptically, 'We now know all about salt-glazing. Or at least that it exists.'

Pot Shots was a special enterprise, fraught with great pleasure, but the peak experience for me came off camera on the evening I spent with David Attenborough doing the voice-recording. It was a long session, but when the job was done I mentioned my recent close acquaintance with Arnhem Land. This prompted a wonderful stream of reminiscence about the place and its weird and wonderful creatures. It was, Attenborough thought, 'one of the most amazingly beautiful places on the planet'. Before I stepped into the night I took the liberty of asking the great man whether he had any keen enthusiasms, other than for the world's wildlife. He replied in positive fashion: 'Yes, of course ... er ... no, not really.'

My other main area of unfinished business was puppet disposal. We had almost 1,000 latex *Spitting Image* veterans warehoused in the East End, gathering dust. In consultation with Sotheby's auction house, I decided to tidy up some of the more presentable ones and put them on the open market. Informed opinion had it that they might fetch as much as £100,000, which, even after paying off all dues and expenses, seemed likely to yield a nice little bonus for my two favourite charities – the Hackney Empire Appeal Fund and me. In fact, they realized £370,105.

Bids for the puppets were submitted through the internet, and they came in droves. Margaret Thatcher was the clear winner in the bidding stakes, selling for £11,224 with thirty-nine bids placed on her puppet. Heading the also-rans was Mick 'Big Lips' Jagger at £7,645, with Ronald and Nancy Reagan close behind. The Royal Family also produced a good return with the Queen (£4,383), Prince Philip (£4,496) and Prince Charles sporting a daffodil in his lapel (£3,496) all showing strongly. Elvis Presley topped the pops at £4,162, while George Best (£4,490) headed the list of sports personalities, narrowly edging out Eric Cantona on £4,386. Tony and Cherie Blair attracted a lot of bids but only just topped £3,000, well short of the £4,858 realized by a menacing Norman Tebbit in biker's leathers.

As the bids were made on the internet it was relatively easy for bidders to disguise their identities and make purchases through proxy names. I cannot therefore, hand on heart, claim that all the puppets went to caring, loving and understanding homes. Some it appears were almost certainly snapped by their human lookalikes with the purpose of effecting their total suppression. Either way, I could not complain. I had hoped that the puppet auction would provide me with sufficient funds to buy a house in Bondi and a brand-new boogie board, but now I entertained notions of buying the whole beach.

My enthusiasm for Australia, it must be said, was not wildly applauded by the rest of my family. I think it may have been generally thought that with eight grandchildren growing up in the London area I should have been more content with a slippers and pipe way of going on that gave them greater access to me. At least, this is what I thought my son, Shem, was implying when he insisted on calling me 'the teenage granddad'.

Deirdre, however, probably against her better judgement, was beginning to get a bit intrigued by the possibility of direct acquaintance with a possum. As a result she graciously consented to accompany her spouse, for a trial period at least, on his next flight to Sydney.

CHAPTER SIXTEEN

CHINESE TAKEAWAY

Back in Bondi I was soon embarked on a new career as an art teacher to the local infants. As I had no formal training in the education of people who scarcely reached my shins, you could say this was an opportunistic move on my part, but I prefer to class it as enlightened self-interest.

It all came about as I was looking for a replacement for my wonderfully convenient cell at the arts college where, sadly, my term as 'Artist in Residence' had expired. I needed studio space not only to work in, but as a place where I could dump all my stuff after my trips, and then collate and reference at leisure. While pondering this problem on the sun-kissed beach, I wandered into the Bondi Pavilion, a pleasant if somewhat ramshackle structure, used to host a variety of local events – fêtes, exhibitions and whatnot. And there, in one of its recesses, I saw the perfect space: a well-lit, spacious room housing some stacked boxes, a few large carnival heads and a full-size papier-mâché mermaid, but encouragingly with no sign of human occupancy.

Bondi Pavilion is a municipal edifice, and Waverley Council, the relevant local authority, had no particular interest in renting any of its precincts for private enterprise. However, it was interested in starting up an art class for the hordes of young sprouts who thronged the area during the school holidays. The question was: Was I a fit and proper person to take them on? I was able to assure the project officer of my very keen interest in the young. Moreover, any worries they might have about my Pommy paedophile potential could be obviated by my involving my wife Deirdre, who was not only an arts graduate but a past master of all the arcane child-minding skills like nose-wiping and emergency toileting.

And so the deal was done. During the school vacations I became one of the Bondi Pavilion art masters, and Waverley let me have the space, and permission to store my stuff, for a peppercorn rent. A further fringe benefit was accorded by the fact that my studio was flanked by the main ladies' shower room for the beach. I could work all day with a living frieze of hot and cold running nymphs in view.

I like to think that the kids had a good time in my classes. They learned quickly, and I did too. After one of my early lessons I was called into the office by Arabella, the art class administrator, who told me I had to watch my language. One of the children had taken his painting home and his parents, suitably impressed, had told him that it was very good. The child had apparently replied, 'I know, Roger said it was fucking

227

fantastic.' Thereafter, in the interests of keeping my class and my space, I made a big effort not to get too carried away by my pupils' compositions. But we still had a lot of fun making paintings and models, some of which featured in our annual show which was graced by the Mayor of Waverley who handed out the prizes.

The only significant interruption to this educational idyll was 'the great poo crisis'. Years ago Bondi was famously polluted, and the surfers used to organize marches to put pressure on Waverley Council to get their beach cleaned up. The pressure worked. An elaborate and costly sewage system was installed which effectively made Bondi one of the cleanest popular beaches in Australia. However, it so happened that the entrance to my studio was situated over one of the main sewage junctions. It developed a blockage, and the rising matter effectively depopulated the Pavilion. I knew full well from my infancy as a building worker that there was probably no alternative to a brave man making the descent and dislodging the stuff with his hands. But I was not about to volunteer, and Waverley Council did not appear to have such a man in their employ. Instead, after a long delay, they wheeled up $60,000 worth of electronic equipment with a sophisticated camera attachment to do the job. The electronically controlled camera, operated by a skilled technician, probed down to locate the blockage – and never came up. In the end the day was saved by Waverley's recruitment of two recent immigrants, both obviously keen to ingratiate themselves with the host nation. They went down, did the necessary, and Bondi breathed again.

There are not too many Asians in Australia, but Sydney has quite a few. I had some in my class and I came across even more through my friend and Bondi neighbour, John Pinder, who organized a Sydney Comedy Festival, with a special category of competitions for children. The thing that impressed him, and me, was how totally 'Australianized' a second-generation Asian can be. The children's cartoon competition was won by an 8-year-old Asian girl who submitted a work featuring John Howard, the Australian Prime Minister, brown-nosing George Bush, the American President, and Bush is saying, 'Don't worry John, the bullshit comes out of this end.'

The influence also went the other way. Australians are now great collectors of Asian art and artefacts, and this is much more than a fashion statement. The Asian aesthetic can be seen in the roll call of Australian landscape painters – Fred Williams, John Olsen, Brett Whiteley and Joe Furlonger. Ian Fairweather, a Scot by birth but classed as Australia's first major abstract artist, produced work that was deeply influenced by Chinese calligraphy and brush paintings. The more familiar I became with what had been achieved in Australian art, the more I began to realize the importance of the role played by the proximity of Asia, and in particular China. And the more I wanted to explore this area further.

Then, as luck would have it, I met Ray Hughes, though I already knew something of his legend. Hughes runs a highly successful art gallery in Sydney's Surry Hills, which has exhibited the A to Z of Australian art for decades and a lot more besides. Australians buy a lot of contemporary art because that it is pretty much all they can buy. The best work of deceased blue-chip artists – Arthur Boyd, Sidney Nolan, Whiteley and the rest – has long since been sold to collections. So an ambitious gallery-owner needs to rove wide in the constant quest for interesting stuff to exhibit. To stock his enterprise Hughes lives in almost constant motion, travelling all over the world, leaving an indelible impression wherever he goes.

I have known characters who could eat more than Ray Hughes and writers who drank more than Hughes. I have even known people who smoked more than Hughes. But I have never come across anyone who could combine all three on such a scale and still run a demanding business. The Sydney artist Michael Snape said of Hughes, 'You watch him, the way he lives, and you just wonder how he keeps on living.' Imagine Henry VIII in a battered homburg and rumpled Sidney Greenstreet suit, with braces and a lurid tie Greenstreet would not be seen dead in, and you are getting the picture of Ray Hughes. And like Henry VIII, Hughes firmly believes in the triumph of his own will: 'If they don't like the way I do business they can fuck off and buy art elsewhere until their nose bleeds.'

I could tell we would get along just fine, so it took me less than a millisecond to accept his invitation to tag along on his next buying mission to China. For me the enterprise afforded the prospect of a double delight – seeing the art and getting a close-up of Hughes in action.

Passport control at Beijing airport has a huge video screen flashing up 'Thou Shalt Nots' in Chinese and English. The taxi ride from the airport goes promptly onto my list of 'Shalt Nots' – an adrenaline-soaked nightmare in a mobile matchbox. Ray commandeers the front seat and spends the first half of the journey trying to pull the seatbelt round his girth and the second half trying to find the connection, muttering 'Why don't they put some hair on it?'

A cotton-grey mist that smells and tastes hangs over everything. Beijing is a bleached-out black and white photograph

Ray Hughes

231

spiked with more cranes than I knew existed. You do not have to be in China for more than two minutes to realize that it is going through irrevocable change – political, physical and economic. But how does one get a handle on such drastic changes and their social effects. It is all so big, and the population figure alone (said to be a billion) taxes the limits of my imagination. But Ray, a great believer in moving from the particular to the general, says there is no reason to be daunted. Our trip should open windows on the society that cannot be found in any political or economic textbook. As he put it: 'The artist describes the world in the first person; this is *my* life and *my* experiences. Get twenty-five to thirty talented artists doing that and weave them together and you start to get an idea of their society.'

The Bamboo Garden Hotel, which actually has a bamboo garden complete with birds, is a green oasis and reminder of a China rapidly disappearing under a tidal wave of concrete. The hotel is situated in a small pocket of central Beijing the cranes have yet to demolish. Ray, clearly an honoured guest, is allotted the Ming suite. The plan is that we should rampage through five cities in ten days, with Beijing the focus at the beginning and Shanghai at the end. Ray calculates that we should see the inside of four artists' studios and three restaurants in any given day – art triumphing over gastronomy by a whisker.

Take the Boulevard of Heavenly Peace eastwards and forty-five minutes later you arrive in Song Village, a farming community on the city limits, now colonized by artists, many of whom are on Ray's contact list. First up Fang Lijun, one of the most celebrated and successful of the Beijing group. His gate opens into a courtyard surrounded by a cluster of farm buildings which once housed several families. Like Damien Hirst, Fang

Lijun is essentially an artist–entrepreneur. His workshop employs outworkers to do the boring bits. In his impressive space he executes huge paintings of swimmers and 20-foot high woodcuts. His style is almost comic strip, with great economy of line, typical of traditional Chinese art. It also has a graphic simplicity and power not unlike the cinema posters he cut his teeth on at the beginning of his career.

Ray makes admiring noises, but murmurs to me he's looking for something more offbeat. 'I'm always looking for artists in the wrong place at the right time, people who are different.' Ray thinks the three brothers Luo fit the bill. The brothers all work together on the same paintings and live in a modest Song Village studio complex near by. 'Good morning, comrades,' says Ray, to be informed with grins that 'comrade' is no longer used except as a term of abuse. Ray can't get enough of their witty, high-spirited work and arranges an exhibition for Sydney on the spot with catalogue thrown in. He is told the prices of the paintings and falls silent. 'Are you angry?' enquires the eldest brother. Ray replies, 'I'm not angry.' Roaring with laughter, the brothers explain that he was meant to hear the question: Are you hungry? 'Always,' says Ray and we make our way across the courtyard, over a carpet of corncobs, to the Luos' local hostelry where an immense meal is set before us: roast duck and greens in black bean sauce, several whole fish, an enormous meat pie and what I was told – I do hope unreliably – was sliced donkey dong.

Many of the Beijing artists have studios in new tower blocks with pristine, still functioning lifts. One such studio belongs to Ji Dachun, whose graphite drawings have a distinctive quality. They are stained with patches of colour set in the middle of large blank canvases. I am glad Ray does not ask my opinion as I am not at all sure. Ray has no doubts and two canvases are bought immediately and rolled up to take away.

Ah Xian is another high-rise worker, but his studio is packed with moulds and body casts. The only clear space is the bed, which we take turns to sit upon. Ah Xian somehow manages to commute between Beijing and Sydney, producing excellent work in both cities. He says of his first move to Sydney, back in 1990, 'Here in China my spirit was being crushed to death. In Australia I have peace of mind but I stay focused on my work because in that sunny country you are free to crush your own spirit.' Unfortunately for our mission, all Ah Xian's current work is packed away in wooden boxes ready for transhipment to New York, but we agree to meet again soon in Sydney.

Liu Xiaodong and his artist wife, Yu Hong, live on the outer limits of the city in a comfortable house with a large garden. He has been compared to the British painter Lucien Freud, and on the day of our visit he has one finished canvas. It is a painting of a street funeral in Beijing in muted greys and browns set alight by a violent profusion of swirling colours depicting the funeral flowers. It's a show-stopper. We leave with the promise that Liu Xiaodong's painting will follow Ray to Sydney. He is elated. 'It's hard work to keep waking yourself up after thirty years in this business, but Xiaodong's painting does it for me.'

Next day we set off for Beijing railway station at dawn. The station's newsagent is doing a roaring trade in little booklets with titles like *Be a Good Wife in Just a Minute* and *Good Emotion in Just a Minute*. The culture of instant gratification has arrived; for me as much as anybody, because we are off to see the wonderful wizard of Tianjin, Li Jin, my favourite artist.

Li Jin lives and works in a tower block. He is an ink and wash artist who has taken ancient literati brush painting and

234

Li Jin

given it a contemporary relevance. His sheer skill is revered by all the artists we have met, including Fang Lijun, who told me this story: 'Oh, Li Jin is the real artist. When we were students he would take us drawing in the park. He would set us up and then nonchalantly engage a passer-by in conversation while eating a large apple. After a while he would stop munching and turn the apple around, revealing a caricature of the passer-by he'd made with his teeth.'

Li Jin's studio is crammed with Chinese antiquities, fresh flowers, song birds (not all in cages) and glass bowls full of tiny fish. The man himself is as humorous and charming as his drawings. He has a fine black beard and you are not sure, looking at his animated face, whether he is entertaining you or himself. He is clearly a free spirit. He unrolls two 6-foot scrolls of tables seen from above groaning with Chinese food, some of it still alive. Ray salivates. 'You know, he's not only drawn the prawns, he's drawn the taste.' I have to agree. Ray quickly hoovers up all of Li Jin's recent output to take back to Sydney. Hungry work, and lunchtime finds us in Tianjin's finest restaurant, the Rocky Club, a cross between an English gentlemen's club and a museum of antiques. Li Jin orders oysters and fish, a duck complete with head, pigeons, chicken and pork, all of which arrive artfully arranged and decorated, vegetables, squid and flower tea. These are his scrolls made flesh. Ray, resplendent in voluminous bib, is singing Cole Porter's 'I'm in Heaven' between muffled mouthfuls of gourmet delight.

The 5 a.m. start for Kunming next day is tough, though we have now hired a minibus to accommodate our ever-accumulating freight of fine art. Ray, the progress-chaser, tells me, 'When you do a trip like this it's good to snip a few hours off in the morning and arrive with the day in hand. I know it's rough but it makes time. We are not solicitors' wives you know.'

Kunming is in full colour, sunny and relatively unpolluted, at least compared to Beijing, though the inevitable cranes are nodding away. Most of the local talent is to be found in the Upriver Loft Complex – factory buildings converted to studios and exhibition space complete with club room and bar. We spend most of the morning in the studio of Tang Zhigang, known as the soldier artist. His erect bearing reflects his parentage: father a high-ranking army officer, mother a prison warder. Tang Zhigang's realistic depictions of life in the People's Liberation Army have been adapted to ridicule the legacy of his army background. Ray wants six paintings, and the meal follows the deal.

The afternoon is given over to bargaining for cabbage vases at Kunming antique market where Ray does what he does best by behaving badly. When all else fails, Ray takes a fat wad of money from his shirt pocket and waves it under the vendor's nose while making his final offer, then slides it back into his top pocket and makes to go away. 'They can't let that happen,' he says. 'It's the killer move.'

We later return to the loft complex to call on Liu Jianhua. He is courteous and fashionably dressed, with a manner as smooth as his regulation shaved head. His neat studio has display tables of his ceramics: headless and armless girls lounging around on porcelain sofas and traditional platters, their beautifully glazed cheongsam dresses riding up to expose their thighs. The effect is disconcertingly sexy but empty. His modelling skills are superb but I do not expect Germaine Greer will be investing in Liu Jianhua's *œuvre* when it reaches Sydney.

The last leg of my travels with Ray finds us in the Xing Guo Hotel, located in downtown Shanghai in a walled, landscaped park enclosing twenty-eight villas built in a variety of European styles. Chairman Mao and his Central Committee used to stay here. In reception forties armchairs with antimacassars are lined up like soldiers.

In the morning we are met by Li Liang, the owner of the Eastlink Gallery. Li Liang lived in Sydney for eight years and is laid-back and laconic. His gallery is a 1920s warehouse over-looking Suzhou Creek and its busy barge traffic. Six hundred square metres of cutting-edge art provide Ray and Li Liang with much to discuss until Ray launches into a vitriolic diatribe against installations and video art. 'Art for curators,' he sneeringly calls it.

After lunch we visit Lorenz Helbling's Shanghart Gallery and an exhibition of calligraphy. We learn that the consulates in Shanghai are being moved to be grouped in one location for security reasons, and Helbling has been asked to curate a show of up-to-the-minute Chinese art in the vacated Swiss consulate. We are invited. The exhibition includes performance art, installations, photographs, video art and a few token paintings. The video art collects a big crowd. One video features footage of hysterical American teenagers at a pop concert and hysterical Chinese teenagers at a Cultural Revolution rally of the same vintage, both cut together to the beat of Bryan Adams's 'Summer of '69.'

Before we leave I notice that Ray is doing a deal with the video artist. It dawns on me that Ray's theories on art are carved in stone until he sees something he wants.

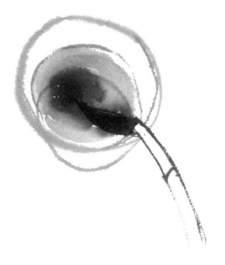

CHAPTER SEVENTEEN

BERK AND WIMP

The Sydney poet, Robert Gray, likens Australia to a halved melon with all its human inhabitants clinging to the rind. It's largely true. You find many Australians in Sydney and Melbourne whose acquaintance with the bush is limited to expeditions that allow them to be home by sundown, in good time for the barbie in their own back yard. They may have previously travelled the world, but knowledge of their own land mass is not among their strongest points.

This was particularly the case with my old *Sunday Times* mate, Tony Clifton, now settled back in his home town of Melbourne after forty years of globetrotting as a war reporter and troubleshooting journalist. Clifton, however, did feel that his ignorance of the outback represented a gap in his education that could, with the enforced leisure of retirement, be repaired. But he is a cautious man – like most surviving war correspondents – and felt the need for company. As it happened, I also wanted to be on the move, if only to test my own vital signs. Not long before I had detected possible symptoms of deafness and dementia. I had misheard George Bush on the radio declaring what I thought was a war on tourism, and found myself nodding in curmudgeonly agreement.

We discussed options. Queensland and the Northern Territory seemed too hot and sweaty, besides which I had already made some inroads in those areas. Western Australia just seemed too vast, Victoria and New South Wales too familiar, and Tasmania too cold and damp – like England with wombats. In the end South Australia, said to contain enough varied wildlife to keep the Discovery Channel busy until the next millennium, more or less chose itself. We even got the South Australian Tourist Board to sponsor our efforts. They seemed to like the concept of two strange old coots exploring strange new territory.

We called ourselves Berk and Wimp after the famous explorers Burke and Wills who charted central Australia and died on their ill-fated expedition of 1861. We planned to start our expedition in Adelaide, then proceed up though the Clare Valley to the Flinders Ranges and Wilpena Pound. We would skirt past Woomera to the opal fields of Coober Pedy, then head east taking in William Creek and Lake Eyre before turning back along the Oodnadatta track to Marree and Parachilna, ending in Adelaide again. It was a tough route, though unlike Burke and Wills we were blessed with a four-wheel drive Landcruiser. As I do not drive, this was perhaps more of an advantage to Berk than it was to Wimp the wheelman, but he had to understand that I, as the illustrator of this adventure, could not waste my valuable time watching the road.

The enterprise began well. Wimp has a knowledge of fine wine, and I had a friend from Cambridge days, Robert Crabtree, who wins prizes for his Rieslings and has a boutique vineyard in the Clare Valley. Clare was named after the Irish county, and we could see why – rolling green hills, small farms, twinkling streams, and settled long enough to have soft pink stone houses, spread far apart in the Celtic manner, and public buildings in the Georgian style. The Jesuits opened the first winery in 1851 to provide altar wine for the new colonies (and are still represented at the Sevenhill Cellars, with Fr John May the winemaker).

The reminder that we were actually in Australia was provided by the birds. Getting up at Clare in the morning is a deafening experience: magpies carol, kookaburras laugh, majestic smoke-grey, chocolate-headed ducks stomp across the grassland, white cockatoos and grey galahs cackle in the gardens, and thousands

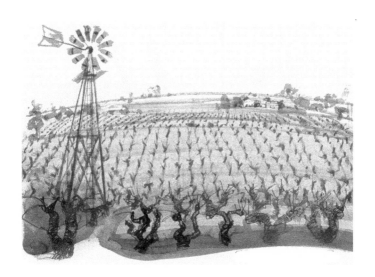

of twittering small emerald-green parrots hang upside down in skeins, like emerald jewellery, from flowering vines. The only drab note was provided by a Pom migrant, a funereal black-bird, fluttering by. It reminded Wimp, who is addicted to metaphor, of 'a vicar avoiding a tart's birthday party'.

There was more majestic stuff, too, of the red in tooth and claw variety. A few miles after leaving Clare our windscreen was darkened by a huge wedge-tailed eagle rising from the roadside bearing a snake caught sunbathing on the tarmac. But what Berk and Wimp thought of as the 'real' Australia did not begin until 100 or so miles north of Clare. The country started to flatten and dry out. The green disappeared and the lush grasses and trees gave way to bare red earth dotted with scrub-by bushes and tussocks of hardy-looking grass – a facsimile of an Aboriginal dot painting. Blue against the horizon were the ridges of the Flinders Ranges, where the geologist Reg Sprigg identified the first signs of multicellular life dating back 600

million years. With dusk approaching we avoided the temptation to branch off towards locations with intriguing sounding names like 'Death Rock' and 'Mount Buggery'. As we neared Wilpena Pound, emus rolled along in single file like hula-hula dancers in grass skirts and the kangaroos bounced along the side of the track as if the bush was a trampoline.

Wilpena Pound is a natural basin ringed by rock outcrops. It is so named because, there being only one narrow gorge entrance, early settlers used it as a natural pound for their cattle *en route* to Adelaide. At the Wilpena Pound Resort, Melissa the barmaid, who looked all of 13 years old, sold us an early morning flight over the Pound along with our drinks. And it was Melissa who greeted us by the airstrip at dawn with the announcement, 'I'm your pilot today.' A very exciting job she did too, while Berk and Wimp held the tiny plane aloft with the cheeks of their buttocks.

Wilpena, from 3,000 feet up, looked like a vast meteor crater

10 miles across, its ridge so wrinkled and fragile it seemed almost too exhausted to hold its shape. The land immediately around the edge is creased like the hide of a giant green dinosaur. Before landing we had to make a low pass over the strip to scare off the kangaroos gambolling on the runway. Back at the resort we encountered German tourists in stout boots, dressed to walk to Darwin, and some stylish Italians in delicate footwear scarcely tough enough to get them as far as the coffee lounge. But no Americans. Osama had frightened them all off.

We were on the empty road to Pimba when I remarked to Wimp that this would be a really bad place to break down. Indeed, there had been a couple of recently reported murders of lone travellers on the route. As if on cue, the dashboard lit up like a Christmas tree, smoke billowed from under the bonnet, the engine died and we slid to a silent stop. A flying stone had cracked the sump and the oil had leaked out. It was over 100° F (38° C) outside, unbelievably hot and extremely lonely.

We got out of the Landcruiser and did what any experienced bushman might do in this situation. We stood in the middle of the road to flag down anything moving and plead for help. I say 'we', but Wimp shrewdly sent me off to sketch in the bush as he thought my resemblance to Ned Kelly's eldest brother might deter other motorists from rendering assistance. Two drivers did generously stop, and within a few hours a pick-up truck arrived. Trustingly, the hire firm let us have a brand new Landcruiser and we were off again to one of Australia's most romantic and mysterious towns, the opal mining centre of Coober Pedy. As we arrived at sunset the worn ridges of the Breakaways, the mountains around the town, looked like the multicoloured surface of an alien planet.

Until 1915 Coober Pedy was a patch of uninhabited rocky desert. That was the year a 14-year-old shepherd boy called Willie Hutchinson picked up what he thought were some coloured marbles. The opal rush began about three minutes after he showed his new-found toys to his dad. The land around Coober Pedy is about as uncomfortable as anywhere on the surface of the planet, with temperatures well over 120° F (49° C) in the summer. To escape the heat the miners dug their houses out of the soft rock in the opal fields, using the mine-shafts for ventilation. They developed a substantial under-ground town, complete with pubs, churches and hotels which are still in use today. The décor is a trendy distressed red with pike and chisel texture. It remains a full-on mining town with its own distinctive golf course – just rock and sand with 'greens' that are black and oil-soaked. Par is 72. We were told that 1989 was a rough year for the golfing community on account of the heavy rainfall which caused grass to grow all over the place. It all had to be cut and rolled flat and dead because nobody knew how to play on the green stuff. They like to play at night with fluorescent balls.

It is still quite a wild town, though with a familiar feel to anyone raised on a diet of old Hollywood westerns featuring Deadwood and Tombstone. Bombings are quite frequent, because explosive material is so readily available. The police station has been bombed twice in the past twenty years, and sundry police cars have disappeared in clouds of smoke. A huge man in a red and black checked shirt confides to us over break-fast, 'If you're going to be a copper around here, you gotta be liked.' For all that, Coober Pedy is a friendly town and not without culture. It has an underground pottery of some distinc-tion run by David Rowe. He told me that he had entered the craft field by way of his conspicuous lack of success as an opal miner. His spouse had delivered an ultimatum – 'Get a life or lose your wife' – and the pottery had been the direct result.

Every resident of Coober Pedy has an opal story. One of the town's leading opal dealers, Yanni Athanasiadis, told us how a nervous young man had come to his shop ten years ago. Yanni produced from his safe a solid block of opal about four inches across and an inch thick in beautiful shades of operatic greens and blues. 'He brought this,' said Yanni. 'Said he hit it by accident on a farm with a post-hole digger while erecting a fence. I gave him $7,000 and told him to bring me the rest. The piece is so big it had to be broken off a seam worth millions. It has to be near here. But the kid never came back. It drives you mad just thinking about it.'

Before opal fever could grab us as fresh victims, we headed off to the more prosaic attractions of William Creek, 100 miles to the east. There had been rain and it was a wonderful drive. The country was dead flat, with a few low trees, but the road was lined with great drifts of flowers. Desert plants are opportunistic and leap out of the ground as soon as a drop of water falls. Clouds of white and yellow flowers reached to the horizon with patches of the aptly named Paterson's curse – a gift to Australia from the same sort of migrant who gave the country rabbits and foxes. In this case a Mr Paterson brought a pretty garden flower related to viper's bugloss from England and planted it at the bottom of his Australian garden. It spread across the country and has been poisoning cattle for 150 years.

William Creek consisted of a roadhouse pub and store with the owner's plane parked outside. The permanent population was three, but half the world seemed to have passed through and left their signatures and other evidence of identity on the pub walls to prove it. Discarded bras, pants and T-shirts also featured, attesting to many a fall-about evening. On the occasion of our visit, a plague of iridescent green stink beetles had descended on William Creek. The pub was packed with drinkers doing two things, getting smashed and stomping the beetles. Stink beetles can emit a reeking spray so they have to be crushed before they can fire. By 1 a.m. the floor was a good

inch deep in beetle juice, but nobody seemed to mind.

The stink of the beetles was pretty rancid, but they smelled like Chanel No. 5 compared to the main attraction, the cat tree. This infamous tree is about four miles from William Creek. From a distance it looked as if it was hung with swarms of bees. Up close the swarms changed to about forty dead cats swinging from the spreading branches. A neat botanical label on the ground in front of the tree reads, 'Pussy Willow (Acacia Felix)'. The cats are not soft little moggies that curl up on your lap but feral mutants literally three or four feet long, mostly ginger or tabbies, with enormous teeth and claws that could have your face off in a trice. They are domestic cats gone wild, fattened by eating the rare local fauna which, until the cat and the fox, had no serious predators. In William Creek we were shown a photo of an eviscerated cat. Its stomach contents were laid out beside it, all virtually undigested, so the bag was a result of one day's hunting. It had killed and swallowed twenty-four painted dragon lizards, three bearded dragon lizards, two earless dragons, three striped skink lizards, one domestic mouse and a zebra finch. The locals obviously love adding to the decorations on the cat tree. In their own bloody way they are serious environmentalists, though they do not take kindly to advice from big-city conservationists. The largest sign in the William Creek pub reads: 'The only true wilderness is between a Greenie's ears.'

Apart from being the only watering hole for many miles William Creek is also the base for visiting Lake Eyre, which is about as far away from it all as you can get in South Australia. Depending on the weather it can be one of the world's biggest inland lakes or the world's largest saltpan (Donald Campbell's land speed record was set there during a dry spell). Wimp and I arranged to fly over its 6,000 square miles – a very disconcerting experience. The lake is so still and heavy with minerals that it acts as a perfect mirror, reflecting back the sky, and this can be particularly worrying when the horizon is lost in a heat shimmer. Our pilot explained that amateur fliers often get into trouble because they cannot tell the lake from the sky. He assured us we were the right way up otherwise our stuff on the floor would be sliding around the cockpit above our heads.

Back on the ground and actually feeling the right way up again, we drove over an arid and desolate stretch of road, the Oodnadatta track, to Marree. It was a long drive but I was able to beguile Wimp with my singing of 'You Are My Sunshine' which he likened to 'the sound of a constipated elephant seal straining over its morning motion'. I was of course only testing to see if his gift for metaphor had been blunted by his long, gruelling hours at the wheel. Clearly it was still intact.

Marree was easily the creepiest stop on our trek. It has a population of around 100, but was once much larger. Marree thrived when the railway to Alice Springs ran through it, but had all but died when the line closed. The pub set the mood. It was a massive place built for the railway maintenance men and the camel and bullock drivers who used to pass through. But in the bar it was almost impossible to reach the counter. The locals had drawn up a semicircle of chairs which effectively fenced out strangers. Seeing what he thought was an opening, Wimp wriggled through to the counter. 'Not there,' said the barman. 'Wet paint.' Uproarious laughter from the local ockers who knew the place had not seen a paintbrush in years.

The Afghan camel drivers who were brought to Australia to open up the central desert areas of the country in the late nineteenth century used to congregate in Marree with their camel trains. The wild descendants of the camels they brought with them are now regarded as among the healthiest camel stock remaining in the world. Unfortunately, Marree has not evolved anything like so well.

The town has made an attempt to turn the Afghan heritage into a tourist attraction by building a rough thatched replica of an outback mosque across from the deserted station. A kindergarten play group has wooden camels for the children to play on. But these seem like token gestures, not at all convincing. Near the few remaining houses that once made up the 'Afghan Town' a frightened woman of Afghan descent told us her kids were being persecuted at school for being Muslims. 'Afghan Town' merely emphasizes how the town was divided as soon as the Afghans arrived. This is also reflected in the old cemetery. The Christians are buried in one corner and the Afghans as far away as possible in another (the Aboriginal dead are even more rigorously segregated). There are about thirty gravestones with a mixture of Arabic and English inscriptions. One read, 'In memory of Wahub, Afghan, died August 1895'. Another, more substantial and suggesting strong integrationist aspirations, was inscribed, 'Mullah Assim Khan, born 1870 Peshawar. Died 1944 Marree, Australia. Loving husband of Agnes, Father of Sheran, Mormin, Emah, Tom, Ali, Zarret, Pat, Aleema, Gloria, Jack and Abdul'.

It is very likely that some of Peshawar-born Mr Khan's children are still alive, but it was hard to imagine them having an outstandingly good time in modern Australia. After George Bush declared his war on terrorism Australia sent its troops into Afghanistan to help trounce the Taliban. However, refugees from that appalling regime who tried to start a new life in Australia found themselves accommodated in a concentration camp located not far away from Marree, in Woomera, previously renowned for its rocket site. It would emerge that many of them had been driven crazy by the heat, the isolation and their treatment there. There were hunger strikes and some sewed up their lips as an expression of protest against the conditions.

These dire events came later, but I did mention to Wimp at the time that the experience of migrants from the Afghan part of the world, past and present, did not seem to sit well with the image of an exuberantly happy multicultural society projected by the Sydney 2000 Olympics. Wimp, who had been a classy 800-metre runner in his youth, would not entertain much criticism of the Olympics, but acknowledged that they may have masked some of the more authoritarian tendencies in his native tradition. 'It's not,' he said, 'the Australian descendants from convicts you have to worry about, it's the descendants of the warders.'

We were glad to shake the red dust of Marree off our feet

and move on. Further down the track we encountered an isolated refuelling stop which also did a nice line in bumper stickers bearing the message, 'I must be immortal, I survived Marree.'

Parachilna, the last stop on our journey, was a lot more life-enhancing. It has a permanent population which we were told 'fluctuated between four and five' but its Prairie Hotel is equipped to cater for the appetites of many miles around. We encountered the 'Feral Mixed Grill' there, a vast platter that for $24 got you kangaroo fillet, camel sausage, emu skewer, goat chop, bacon and mashed potatoes. On the hotel wall was a poster inviting the surrounding district to 'The Woolbalers Bachelors and Spinsters Ball'. All comers were advised: 'There's a shitload of drench which needs to be consumed. 10,000 cans of rum in fact. We need you. But if you cannot stand the pace, stay in your paddock.'

Enriched by these experiences, Wimp reverted to the persona of Tony Clifton and returned to Melbourne where he vowed to tell his sophisticated chums about what an extraordinarily weird and wonderful country they were all living in. Back in Sydney, down by the harbour, I was telling a friend about my trip to South Australia when I was interrupted by a chipper old lady. 'I'm from South Australia,' she said. 'What did you think of it?' I said I thought it was terrific as long as you are not an Afghan or an Aboriginal. 'Shit yeah,' she said. 'Australia's a great country as long as you behave yourself.'

CHAPTER EIGHTEEN

WALKABOUT

Of all the hostels I've frequented, the Last Resort in Broome on the west coast of Western Australia was the most memorable. It was conveniently close to the airport which featured light air-craft trips over the shoreline, and many of its customers were heavily into free-falling. It was like being in an RAF mess *circa* 1940, with the cheering difference that most of the clientele came back. The structure was wooden and the facilities were rudimentary; the kitchen could only have been improved by a scud missile attack. There was also the problem of the music, high-decibel until late into the evening. But the company was friendly and the bill was charitably low.

I had been pointed in the direction of Broome by none other than Lord Alistair McAlpine, Mrs Thatcher's party fund-raiser and a renowned Aussiephile whose list of thought-provoking publications included *Once a Jolly Swagman*. A mutual friend had suggested that I ring him, and McAlpine was wonderfully informative. If I wanted to know where to make a start in Western Australia's vast expanse of territory, he thought I could not do better than Broome which had a history as well as a modern appeal. The harbour area had been first spotted by William Dampier, the pirate explorer, in 1699, many years before Captain Cook clapped eyes on the continent. But its real eminence came in the 1870s with the development of the pearl fishing industry. In more recent years there had, Lord McAlpine told me, been some impressive new building developments. One of them I discovered was the Cable Beach Hotel, built, as chance would have it, by Lord McAlpine.

On arriving in Broome I took a good look at the Cable Beach Hotel, fashioned in a pleasing Asian style with a complement of swimming pools and tennis courts, and checked into the Last Resort. By now you could say I was addicted to hostels. For a man who does not drive (and indeed for a man or woman who does) the hostel network offers the best method of engaging with Australia. Their pin boards and information desks are rich with useful stuff about where to go and where to avoid; how get a lift by subsidizing someone else's petrol, and how to contact resourceful outfits with names like 'Billy Can Tours'. The hostels are also the best grapevine for all the local gossip. With YHA membership (open to all ages), a backpack (complete with tube of Bushman's insect repellent) and a McCafferty's bus timetable, I found that much more freedom of movement was possible than I could have imagined. You can even run into a limo service. On my first trip to the outback in Queensland the hostel picked me and my belongings up at the bus station: my backpack never actually made it onto my back.

Broome's delights are accessible on foot, though a bicycle

helps. There are many sights to see, but it is hard to beat people-watching. The cheap labour the pearling industry required came from Japan, China, Malaya and the Philippines. They met up with the Irish and the poorer Anglos and the indigenous Aboriginals (Aboriginal women were deemed the best pearl divers). This assortment of nationalities has over the years produced a most exotic mix.

There is still a whiff of the frontier spirit about the place. The houses, mostly Asian style, are all lattice-work and equipped with verandas. Like Marree, its cemeteries show evidence of segregation, but the ones in Broome have a distinct charm. The Oriental cemetery features many gravestones fashioned from seashell-encrusted rocks pulled from under the sea. The texture of these stones, combined with the decorative calligraphy, creates an effect that is really quite beautiful.

The big attraction, however, is 'The Staircase to the Moon', which is a magnet for tourists. The phenomenon occurs in the spring when the moon is full and is reflected across the mudflats at low tide. With the cover of nightfall it creates a magical Jacob's Ladder effect best witnessed from Broome's Town Beach. I was almost as impressed by Broome's Sun Pictures with its billing 'See the Stars under the Stars'. A success since its opening night in 1916, it may be the world's oldest outdoor cinema. The movie screen has to vie for attention with dramatic sunsets, boisterous cicadas and giggling Aboriginal children high in the trees. I saw *Independence Day* there, and the bit in the movie where a gigantic spaceship descends on New York coincided with a roaring jet skimming low over the cinema with that day's consignment of backpackers. I almost died of fright.

I ventured further up the coast to Derby as part of an organized tour. No organized trip in Australia is ever complete without going to jail. They like to show visitors, especially Pommies, what survives of the prison facilities from a not-so-distant past. This is understandable given the nation's heritage, but you do occasionally get the feeling that having seen one lock-up you've seen them all. There can, however, be no such complaint about the one outside Derby. It is an immense hollow Boab tree where malefactors from the outback were held *en route* to the courtroom. Other reminders of modern Australia's rugged origins can be found in Broome's excellent little museum which exhibits an impressive array of neck-chains and leg-irons.

One morning I pedalled over towards Roebuck Bay, about 12 miles east of Broome. Down a rough track I came across the Broome Bird Observatory and Research Centre, where I was told I could have a new species named after me if I was prepared to donate upwards of $2,500 to the Western Australia Museum. I took a rain-check on this kind offer and pedalled on. I'm glad I did. What struck me was how the same elements you can see on any English coastline could be so vividly different in Australia. Roebuck Bay exhibits mile after mile of sparkling green mudflats. The pebbles on the beach were black, the sand red and the sea was a milky turquoise teeming with all manner of weird wildlife – too spooky for swimming. I happily settled for spending the day drawing the energetic mudskippers while Aboriginal fishermen pulled barramundi out of the mangrove shallows.

My trip to Broome allowed me to make the modest boast that I had sketched and painted in all the mainland states of Australia. And I did feel privileged. In England it is very hard to paint anywhere without getting the feeling that what you are looking at has already been copyrighted by Turner or Constable. And if they have not been there before you, you can be sure that Norman Ackroyd has. There is virtually no area of the countryside you can depict without feeling that somebody has previously done the job more successfully than you are ever likely to achieve. In Australia, even with its wonderful tradition of outdoor painting by Sidney Nolan and many others, you often get the feeling that its landscape and its strange creatures are revealingly themselves to you personally for the first time. But I was still not entirely satisfied.

In England whenever the need came over me I walked and cycled around North Norfolk from Holkham Estate, through Wells-next-the-Sea to Cromer and back. It never let me down. I always returned to London feeling invigorated. I asked among my Bondi friends whether there was anywhere in this sunburnt continent that was at all like Norfolk, and I gave them a rough idea of what I was looking for. I had to put up with a lot of quips along the lines of, 'Why don't you just go for a walk in a wind tunnel?' But some kind of consensus did emerge in the end: I should try the Coorong.

The Coorong in South Australia is a wetlands with its saline lagoons protected from the sea by the sandhills of the

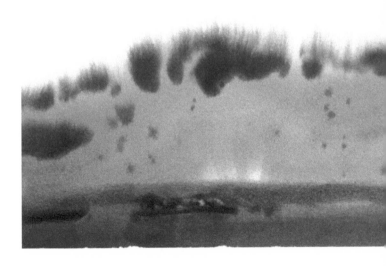

Younghusband Peninsula. In fact, Berk and Wimp had been close to it on their epic tour of the central parts of the state. But instead of going north from Adelaide, you need to head south. Like Norfolk, the Coorong is on the way to nowhere. Keep going and you are sure to fall in the sea.

The Coorong is as damp as the rest of the state is dry. Its wetlands are essentially formed by the Murray, Australia's largest river system, which runs into the southern ocean, south-east of Adelaide. The Murray upstream is bled by countless irrigation areas so by the time it gets to its estuary what remains of its flow is sluggish and loaded with silt. The terrain is fashioned partly by this phenomenon and partly by the wind. In East Anglia the wind cuts through you direct from Siberia. In the Coorong the trees are shaped by wind with a touch of ice straight from Antarctica. The end product is something that looks like old graphic illustrations of the Fens before they were drained, but reproduced in full-colour Cinemascope.

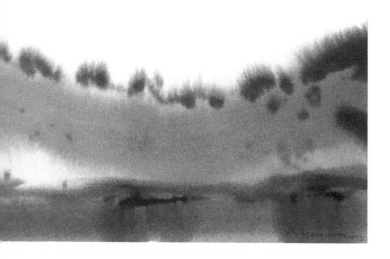

Norfolk is manageable on foot or by bicycle. The Coorong is not. It is just too big. I tried with the bike but it was not possible to cover the ground. Thirty miles out from a hostel often meant thirty miles back again for want of useful facilities along the way, like pubs. I did come across a remote general store equipped with a warning sign, 'No cash. No booze', but I did not feel I could reliably come across another. Place names like 'Ninety Mile Beach' did not occur for no reason.

Eventually I solved the problem by basing myself in the estuary port of Goolwa. I was comfortably accommodated in *The*

Murray River Queen, a paddle-steamer berthed in its namesake river. It had fifty-two cabins, but as it was out of season I was the only paying guest. At night I felt like a Mississippi gambler with no one to play cards with. From Goolwa I was able to advance my knowledge of the region by taking trips, most of them with David Dadd of Coorong Nature Tours who showed me sights of a type not witnessed in Norfolk. One remarkable lagoon he drove me to was an exquisite rose madder in colour. The next was a spectacular milky white dotted with black swans like a crazed musical score. Without beating every bush we managed to see sixty-seven different species of birds in one day. While keeping one hand loosely on the wheel of his Land Rover, Dadd introduced me to whistling kites and straw-necked ibises, Caspian terns down from Russia for their summer holidays, pallid cuckoos and stubble quail, whiskered terns and black-winged stilts. My personal favourite was the royal spoonbill, a real aristocrat, but the Coorong signature bird is the pelican. Parliaments of these birds congregate in the offshore inlets, never far from a fisherman's rod and line. They sometimes overpopulate their feeding grounds and have been known to work in pairs mugging people coming out of coastal fish shops. Dadd indulgently saw this as a fitting reversal of history as the early settlers were prone to canning the wildlife. Tinned black swan was sold as 'Robe goose'. The cannery failed, however, as the tins had a disconcerting habit of exploding.

Aside from the landscape and its creatures, Dadd was himself an interesting study. Originally from the sparrow-infested wetland of the Isle of Dogs in London's East End, Dadd achieved his exalted status in the Coorong after many years operating the Narrung ferry between Lakes Alexandrina and Albert. Birds were his speciality, but he had a treasure trove of stories about many other aspects of natural history. Did I know, for example, that hairy-nosed wombat poo was four times drier than that of a camel? Or that the Tasmanian tiger kept his testicles in a pouch? These little nuggets have stuck in my memory, though it is just possible that they were products of a mickey-taking Cockney imagination rather than copper-bottomed facts. Either way, they enlivened my experience of the Coorong.

It was through Dadd that I had the rewarding experience of

meeting Henry Rankine, a tribal leader of the Ngarrindjeri people who had a rough time of it when white settlers first arrived in the Coorong. Rankine himself can remember the days when Aboriginals were barred from restaurants and 'you could go to jail for three months if you had a beer'. Nowadays Rankine is a highly respected citizen and a Justice of the Peace, though the experience of dispensing justice still seems a bit novel: 'Most black people face the bench, they don't sit on it.'

Rankine is a great story-teller about matters ancient and modern. He naturally had a legend explaining the curious appearance of the Coorong. One of his ancestors, a great warrior, had chased a giant Murray cod down the river when it was only a tiny stream. Their epic battle had gouged out the river bed, throwing up the islands and the sandbanks that now make up the land mass. The giant cod was eventually caught and cut up into pieces which were thrown back into the water and grew into the fishes of today.

From the realms of legend we moved on to my mentioning some of the parallels between Norfolk and the Coorong. This led to comparisons of methods of obtaining sustenance from the land. Rankin wondered if I knew about the method his tribe used to trap the succulent Cape Barren geese. It went like this: 'The men would be naked, and they'd get down and crawl backwards into the flock of geese. And the geese would be so astonished, that they'd forget to fly, and come to have a closer look, and then they'd grab them.' I had to concede that our trapping skills in Norfolk never managed to achieve this level of sophistication.

CHAPTER NINETEEN

HOME AND AWAY

I suppose some part of me always knew that my past would catch up with me. As I may have mentioned, the end of the *Spitting Image* period was perhaps the most blessed relief of my existence. I was, at least on any conscious level, totally immune to any suggestion that the show might be revived. Then, in the autumn of 2003, I heard word that John Lloyd, the programme's first producer, was planning to come out of his long self-imposed purdah and relaunch *Spitting Image* for the benefit of the twenty-first century. I then heard from John himself: Would I come and help out?

To say I was torn would be a massive understatement. I knew that Lloyd, as the man who had saved the original show by actually making it funny, could do the job, if anyone could. It also appeared, even from the vantage point of my boogie board on Bondi Beach, that the Blair regime in Britain was suffering grievously from an acute lack of savage satirical attention. At the same time I dreaded the prospect of abandoning my Aussie idyll and going back into showbiz mode with all those gut-wrenching deadlines. But there was another prospect, equally dire. Supposing the show did manage to relaunch in some style with me sidelined on the other side of the planet, as the forgotten man of *Spitting Image*. How would I feel then? Not good, I concluded. I therefore decided to check the thing out at closer range.

I was lucky in the sense that I was due for another English interlude. It was time for me to bear gifts again and conduct a fresh census of my grandchildren. I was relieved to find there were still only eight. I also wanted to test the London art market with a view to unloading another portfolio of work from the Australian outback. And there was another long-unresolved matter in England that required my attention relating to a barn.

In the last days of *Spitting Image* Mark 1, I had used part of my ill-gotten gains to acquire a derelict barn on the North Norfolk coast. This had been undergoing what seemed like an interminable conversion. The original idea was that, once converted, it would provide a holiday hideaway by the sea for all the grandchildren far from their unhealthy natural habitats on the mean streets of North London. They had acquired buckets and spades in anticipation of this happy prospect back in 1997, all now rusty with disuse. Six years on, the barn was still a building site.

My initial duties in relation to *Spitting Image* Mark 2 were fairly rapidly discharged. I had to canvass all the child-labourers who had worked in the original sweatshop and test their motivation in relation to a new challenge. I felt a bit like the old, bald geezer in *The Seven Samurai* who went round recruiting his young mates for one last lunatic enterprise. Most of the child-labourers were now of course in their thirties with wives, children, mortgages and, in some cases, mistresses to support. These impediments notwithstanding, they were, almost without exception, up for it. It really is amazing how addictive stress can be.

My next task, carried out with Richard Bennett, *Spitting Image*'s long-time and long-suffering financial director, was to put together a proposed budget for the enterprise. We gave our findings on this subject to John Lloyd who, in turn, sent them on to ITV and the show's potential backers. Then, as is customary in these matters, we had to sit and wait while the higher bean-counters did their own sums. And then wait some more while they checked them out.

Fortunately my other projects provided me with adequate diversion in the meantime. My trawl of the London galleries with my Australian paintings and drawings eventually got a green light from The Fine Art Society in New Bond Street. It was very nice that my stuff would be exhibited in exalted company with the likes of William Nicholson, Frank Brangwyn, Edward Bawden and John Byrne, though I still had some way to go before overhauling my old mate David King. The extraordinary collection of Russian revolutionary photographs and posters King had built up over the years had come to occupy a room of its own at Tate Modern. He just loved showing me around. The work was so cunningly arranged by the man himself that Leon Trotsky's eyes seemed to follow us all over the room.

Going the rounds of the galleries I was impressed by the number of new ones that had sprung up in the East End during my absence, and especially by the Prince's Drawing School in Shoreditch which kindly asked me to give a talk. I found that Catherine Goodman, the school's entrancing artistic director, had also been tutored by Ed Middleditch, the man

Law and Lloyd

who originally propelled me in the direction of the Royal College. Middleditch, it will be recalled, was the man under whose stern gaze I was obliged to repeatedly draw the same galvanized tin bucket. However, his teaching methods were apparently a lot more flexible than I had suspected. The comely Ms Goodman remembered Middleditch best for his habit of reciting poetry to her while she painted.

The Drawing School also provided me with a memorable evening which brought certain aspects of my English and Australian experiences together. The occasion was the première of a film about the artist Lucien Freud. It was put together by Jake Aubach and the art critic William Feaver, a good friend who wrote the uplifting programme notes for my *Aussie Stuff: Way Beyond the Black Stump* exhibition some years earlier. The film consisted of many enlightening interviews with the people who had sat for Freud over the years. These included some of his daughters and a succession of girlfriends who provided insights into the great painter's methods. In arty circles it was the hot ticket of the season.

Shortly before the screening took place I was informed that Ray Hughes, Sydney's art dealer extraordinaire, was in town and eager to be invited. I fixed it with William Feaver and at the appointed time Ray lurched ominously into view. The lights went down on the assembled artistic glitterati and the film started, accompanied by an unscripted declaration made in a thick Queensland accent, 'This is just like evenings I used to give in Brisbane Town Hall.' Soon the reverential voices of Lucien Freud's reminiscing friends and lovers were interrupted by the sound of Ray toppling forwards off his chair and sprawling headlong on the floor. Somehow he had managed to get the chair caught up between his body and coat. This made the business of extricating him and getting him safely rebalanced a difficult and noisy process. Matters then quietened down a bit as

Ray nodded off and only snored within reason. After the show Feaver generously waved aside my apology for my Australian friend's performance art. 'It could,' he said, 'only have been Ray.'

These forays into London for artistic encounters were, however, isolated occurrences. Most of my time was spent on the North Norfolk coast in the barn. I would like to relate that it was my childhood experience as an ace boy builder that accelerated matters there, but I don't think that counted for very much. However, my glowering presence on site did seem to provide the builders with that little extra bit of motivation. They just couldn't wait to get away from me and on to the next site.

The barn conversion was completed by the early summer. As soon as the new lavatories flushed, a people carrier arrived outside and decanted four grandchildren (each with a friend), assorted parents and a dog called Rosie. They announced their intention of staying for the entire summer, and courteously evicted Deirdre and myself, though we were allowed to hang out in the barn's studio next door.

Soon afterwards I got news about *Spitting Image*. The proposed budget had gone through the wringer with ITV and the production company involved in the deal and had come back with some interesting amendments. Under the scrutiny of the higher bean-counters, the amount of what is known in the trade as 'How's it going' money – as in 'How's it going and where's my cheque?' – had incredibly gone up, but only at the expense of funds for actual puppet production. I was charmed to see my name on the 'How's it going' list of beneficiaries, but I did not see how a half-decent show could be reassembled on such a lop-sided basis. There was also no money earmarked for a pilot programme, which I thought was absolutely essential to get the ring-rust out of our system before going on air. From my point of view (and not long after from John Lloyd's), *Spitting Image* Mark 2 had turned out to be a sodden squib. By now thoroughly surplus to requirements, Deirdre and I sloped off back to Bondi.

Deirdre's trial period with me in Australia had now gone on for so long that I was beginning to suspect she might actually like the place, even if she still maintained reservations about her spouse. It is possible this was a result of my taking her round to some of the edited high spots of my earlier walkabouts. Thus I returned to Broome in Western Australia with her where we experienced the thrill of movie-going under the stars at Broome Sun Pictures. But the expedition that we both enjoyed most was the return to Cunnamulla with the Aboriginal writer Herb Wharton, now an old mate, as our mentor and guide.

The high-minded purpose of the trip was to develop my acquaintance with the Queensland bilby, which I was eager to draw from life. The bilby is a marsupial, a member of the bandicoot family, with a passing resemblance to a rabbit. It has an almost iconic status among Australia's rarer species, and as a direct result there are no end of chocolate bilbies. Darrell Lea, the confectionery company which produces most of them, responsibly donates a percentage of its sales to a Save the Bilby Fund. So the bilby has a high public profile, but you do not see many of them around, not even in Queensland. There were said to be only 800 left in the wild, though there were some in captivity within striking distance of Cunnamulla which, with the help of Herb Wharton's connections in the bilby conservation business, we had some prospect of seeing.

The bilby quest began to take on a biblical aspect when, driving up from the south, we encountered a plague of locusts at Nyngan. Locusts will eat anything green, including your shirt. At dusk the locusts swirled in the hot wind like snow. Outside the car we discovered they are crunchy underfoot, again not unlike snow. Driving at dusk in the outback can be a stop-and-go process as it is the time of day when kangaroos develop a suicidal tendency to leap out of the bush in front of any fast-moving objects.

Next morning we drove into Cunnamulla to the strains of Slim Dusty's song 'Cunnamulla Fella' on our car radio. Herb was there to greet us. He told me that the last man to be hanged in Queensland was, in fact, a Cunnamulla fella. He had robbed the bank and made it away with the cash but his horse bolted off in fright, leaving him stranded in the main street. Forced to leg it, he eventually found what he thought was secure concealment up a tree. But the local cops outwitted him by tracking his dog which, loyal to a fault, came panting eagerly up to the robber's leafy hiding place and then sat barking its love up into the

Herb Wharton

tree. 'Disorganized crime,' Herb concluded, 'definitely does not pay.'

Cunnamulla was much as I remembered it from seven years earlier, though the trees in the town centre were a little taller. But it was summer, not spring, and oppressively hot even with a breeze – a bit like being in a fan oven at gas mark 8. We were in no mad rush, so we decided to head over to Eulo to see how things were going there. First up was a visit to Nan and Ian Pike's Date Farm and Winery. On my previous trip the enterprise was in its unformed infancy, but now it was clearly moving smoothly upmarket.

Eulo has artesian mud springs rich in minerals, and Ian Pike had installed mud baths in the palm grove, indoor and outdoor. When we arrived it was so hot the green tree frogs, who like nothing better than hanging out in a bathroom, were getting sunburned and turning brown. Pike was hard at work on a 'stretch' model – two cast-iron baths, with the ends cut off, welded together to make one huge double so couples could share the muddy experience. He told me, 'The magnesium sulphate in the mud makes you come out looking twenty years younger.' I was impressed, but not entirely convinced. I could not help remembering that the last time I was in Eulo I had lost a packet on a lizard called 'Eternal Youth', so I had built-in immunity to the promise of remedies against old age.

We walked across to the Lizard Race Track, where a large papier-mâché frilled lizard still announced the World Famous Lizard Racing Championships. Sadly, we were told that lizard racing was undergoing something of a decline, a consequence of new drink-driving penalties deterring the high-rollers from out of town. There was no lizard racing on that day, but I did notice a touching monument by the side of the track which I must have missed on my earlier visit. It commemorated 'Destructo', the racing cockroach from Bondi, accidentally stepped on after winning the challenge cup against the champion lizard 'Wooden Head' on 22 August 1981.

Next day we got into some serious bilby action by driving over to the wildlife centre at Charleville. On the car radio we heard a local programme on spouse abuse which concluded with a helpline number which listeners were advised to ring 'to fine tune your relationship'. I could tell the trip was going well as Deirdre did not even bother to note it down. At Charleville we were met by Steve Peck of the Queensland Parks and Wildlife Service, a huge, heavily bearded man who bore an uncanny physical resemblance to the *Guardian* cartoonist Steve

Bell. As it turned out, he also had a droll, Bell-like sense of humour. His passion, he told me, was not for bilbies, but for snakes who regard bilbies as a tasty snack. He rather resented the fact that bilbies got so much public attention while Australia's wonderfully venomous snake varieties – unrivalled throughout the planet – had to go cap in hand for funding.

Despite his reservations about the bilby, Peck proved a goldmine of information about the creature's strange customs and practices. Like all Australian marsupials bilbies are deeply nervous. Their habitat had dwindled with the receding of the Queensland plains. To appease the cattle, large areas are now covered in buffle grass, which insects are not very keen on. This is tough on bilbies, whose preferred diet features cockroaches, grasshoppers, locusts and termites. The Queensland bilbies that remain in the wild are all in Astrebla, an arid area eight hours' drive from Charleville. For the most part, cats, dogs and foxes find Astrebla too harsh for comfort. Even so, a cat shot there recently weighed 12 pounds and its stomach contained a bilby and three dunnarts.

During the day bilbies live beneath the ground in spiral burrows, and to conserve energy they withdraw all the blood from their large ears until they lie crumpled on their heads. The male and female live separately and, given their dwindling numbers, they can have difficulty in locating each other for romantic encounters. However, little time is wasted after they get together. The gestation period is a mere fourteen days, and bilbies have two litters a year (one or two a litter). The young are the size of a jelly bean and live in the female's backward-facing pouch until old enough to venture out. The males have two tusks 2 centimetres long and are exceedingly cunning. Very hard to catch.

The few males they do manage to snare are brought into Charleville's wildlife centre to breed and are later released back into the wild wearing a radio collar. There are no trees in Astrebla so the rangers set up their radio mast on top of a shed. A wedge-tailed eagle immediately built a nest in it and at night the dingoes circled the shed hoping one of the chicks would fall out of the nest. Life in Astrebla is tough for all species. In contrast, life for a bilby at the centre is privileged. The captive-bred bilbies are nurtured in air-conditioned maternity hutches.

The high point of my trip came when Steve Peck reached into one of the hutches and handed me a contented rabbit-sized female with fine silver blue hair, eyes like blackcurrants and a black tail with a white brush at the tip. Slowly her ears unfolded as she woke up and held my melting gaze. Even the snake-loving Peck was moved by the emotion of the occasion.

The next stop for the bilbies bred in captivity will be Queensland's Currawinya National Park. Peck told us that a 15 square mile fenced enclosure was being prepared for them there. The bilbies would move in just as soon as the feral animals living within its precincts had been removed.

There is nothing an Aussie likes better than a fence. You see them all over the country. Every Australian state has rabbit-proof fences. If you include private structures, Queensland alone has 31,000 miles of fencing. Most of these fences fail in their objectives but they make a fine sight stretching for mile after straight mile into the outback. In recent years solar-powered electric fences have become all the rage. The most notorious fence was the 8,000 volt effort built by John Howard's government in Woomera to help protect the indigenous population from the enclosed Iranian and Afghan asylum seekers. The bilbies were also destined to have an electric fence, but its purpose was more benign.

We decided to drive over to Currawinya to observe work in progress. Conveniently, Herb had a nephew, Kenny, a former rodeo rider and bull-riding champion like his uncle, living

locally. Kenny's wife Carmel offered to drive us there in their ute (utility vehicle). Even more conveniently, Herb had another nephew, Danny, who worked as a park ranger in Currawinya with special responsibility for fence maintenance and feral control.

In the course of the day Herb pointed out the bunkhouse where he started his working life, aged 12, in the cattle-droving business. It was now a blackened ruin, but it prompted a vein of reminiscence about early pay days which consisted of a packet of tea and sugar. Kenny and Danny have not had it so hard, but they all feel the Aboriginals still have some way to go in terms of economic and citizenship status. Herb says you can get some idea of how officialdom views them from the fact that the Minister for Aboriginal Affairs is also the minister for immigration policy, whichever party is in power.

It was another blistering day and we stopped for a swim in the Paroo River before taking lunch under the shade of a Coolibar tree while Danny regaled us with feral tales. It seems that the goats are by far the most successful feral creatures in the Currawinya National Park. They eat anything and are amazingly healthy. The rangers put out contracts out on them at $60 a head, but they keep coming back. Deirdre was pleased to see that the fenced enclosure set aside for the incoming bilbies was refreshingly feral-free. She could tell they were going to a good home.

CHAPTER TWENTY

NO WORRiES

When I first thought of coming to Australia I imagined I was taking a step back from the modern world. How thoroughly mistaken can a man get? In mitigation I can only plead that this was in the dark ages before the 2000 Olympics and before the world took to renewing itself every New Year's Eve through telecast witness of the eruption of fireworks over the Sydney Opera House.

Now of course Australia is recognized as the acme of stylish modernity, its lifestyle and culture widely celebrated throughout the planet. Its authors, actors and artists enjoy a prominence once only available to its athletes. British celebrities queue up for the honour of being humiliated in its rainforests. Travel magazines laud it as a destination where you can get suitably sun-kissed and broaden your intellectual horizons at the same time. Critics of the place are now, as they say in this newly sophisticated environment, as rare as rocking-horse shit.

In the 2004 Boyer Lectures (Australia's equivalent of the Reith Lectures) the erudite Tasmanian-born author and critic, Peter Conrad, advanced the following propositions: 'Australia has, after the centuries of rejection, won the role of wish-fulfilment fantasy ... The British public spends its time fantasizing about a holiday or the chance to emigrate there.' Conrad's thesis was that Australia had recently come to occupy the status of a utopia in the imagination of its beholders, particularly 'miserable Britons'. He could, however, have broadened the argument to include once-miserable Aussies, the ones who fled the country of their birth, deeming it a cultural desert, but who are now returning in droves.

Among the most recent returnees has been Murray Sayle, the journalist who most enlivened my days at the *Sunday Times* back in the late 1960s and early 1970s, before he took off for Japan. Sayle finally descended from his perch on the slopes of Mount Fuji to give his homeland another once-over when his student children allocated him and his wife Jenny a bed in their Sydney abode. I found him there working on a laptop on a corner of the kitchen table hemmed in by student debris and looming deadlines. He told me he was in the process of tracking down his first girlfriend (who had to be at least 82), not for romance, but to fill him in on how things had changed. One of his problems in getting a handle on events was that most his contemporaries were dead or 'had one foot in the grave and the other on a banana skin'. His impression was that the place had changed for the better, but he was reserving judgement about the people, who seemed 'to spend too much time reassuring themselves that they are wonderful'. But, on balance, he seemed inclined to stick around.

Indeed, all the energetic Aussies I first met on the *Sunday Times* have now, with one notable exception, come back to live in Australia, though Nelson Mews, once the doyen of current affairs programmes at London Weekend Television, has probably rendered himself more inaccessible by living on a boat berthed upriver from Perth. My other old newspaper mates, Tony Clifton in Melbourne and Alex Mitchell in Sydney, sometimes come out to play, when their schedules allow. And I am indebted to Mitchell's wife Judith White for extending my acquaintance in the Australian artistic community. She works for the Art Gallery of New South Wales, and kindly arranged for me to give a talk there. Any doubts I had about it being coincidentally scheduled for the day after the destruction of the Twin Towers evaporated after Judith's skilful introduction defused the situation.

Even the one exception, Phillip Knightley, maintains a flat in Sydney and is often seen at fashionable parties in the harbour area. A prolific author, Knightley expiates his guilt for still having Notting Hill Gate as his main domicile by writing articles with headlines like 'Australia, why ever did I leave you?' He rationalizes his position by echoing Barry Humphries's thoughts on the subject: 'I've suddenly discovered that England is a province of Australia.' This enables him to claim he has not left home after all.

I do not find myself begrudging an element of Aussie jingoism, though the level of self-congratulation can sometimes, as Murray Sayle suggests, be a bit over the top. After all, no country that elects John Howard for a third term as its Prime Minister can be all good. Despite my long absence from the caricaturist's bench I still find it impossibly difficult not to judge political leaders by their faces, and Howard's, which appears to seamlessly combine elements of foxiness and petulance, is less than inspirational. I cannot help feeling that a more benign countenance is required to deal with the nation's delicate racial situation. Though the all-out 'white Australia' ethos has had its day, it is clear from the plight of the country's Third World asylum seekers, not to mention that of indigenous Aboriginals, that there is deep confusion about how off-white it is prepared to be.

However, the racism that you encounter in Australia, even in redneck territory, seems to lack the malevolent edge that is still sometimes manifest in the American South and in parts of London's East End. Dissent from prevailing racial attitudes can earn you some uncomfortable moments in outback pubs, but your chances of getting out alive are relatively good. You get the feeling that Australia has the ability to surmount its problems in this area, as it has done in so many others.

I am not entirely thrilled by Australia becoming so fashionable because I know only too well from the *Spitting Image* experience that fashions invariably change. On the other hand, it does seem to have underlying qualities that are likely to endure, if only because its extraordinary landscape cuts all human pretensions down to size. And the egalitarian spirit which D.H. Lawrence conveyed so brilliantly in *Kangaroo* back in 1923 still maintains its resilience. 'There is all the difference in the world,' wrote Lawrence, 'between feeling better than your fellow men, and merely feeling better off.' Australia undoubtedly feels even better off than it did then, but it is unlikely to get totally carried away with itself.

Meantime I am very happy to stay on, drawing and painting its inexhaustible supply of landscape and wild creatures, using the Bondi Beach studio as a base for operations. I should also mention that perceptions of me as a 'teenage granddad' have, like those of Australia, changed for the better though perhaps not quite so dramatically. The oldest of the grandchildren is very insistent about coming to Bondi for her imminent 'gap

year'. I am also reliably informed that this contagion is spreading fast down the ranks. The way things are shaping up in the family, it looks as if Deirdre and I are going to be stuck out here in utopia for some time to come.

ACKNOWLEDGEMENTS

I am indebted to Lew Chester, without whom this book would not have been written. This is our third collaboration. Next time Lew will draw the pictures and I'll write the words. Also to Richard Bennett who made it possible for me to run away to Australia and to Rebecca Hossack for getting me there.

In England my thanks also go to John Kelly whose abrasiveness produces pearls, Trevor Dolby and his team at Harper Collins who nagged me not once, Shem Law for answering endless questions and Judith Chester for advice on the script.

And in Australia I am very grateful to Herb Wharton, whose mob have lived in Oz around 50,000 years, for telling me about magical places and to Margie Brown who took me to some of them. Also to Philip Engelberts (South Australian Tourism

Commission) who made the trip to South Australia possible, to Tony Clifton who shared the adventure with me (and whose notes I stole) and to David Dadd (Coorong Nature Tours) for wonderful days in the Coorong. I greatly appreciate the help of Alex Mitchell whose memory of our days at the *Sunday Times* is better than mine and Murray Sayle's permission to quote from *A Crooked Sixpence*, also all the girls at Bondi Pavilion, especially Roz Newton, for the best studio location in the Southern Hemisphere and Deirdre Amsden for her consistent help. Oddly enough, she is still my wife.

BiBLIOGRAPHY

Peter Conrad: *At Home in Australia* published by Thames and Hudson, 2003.

Granta 70: *Australia: The New New World* published by Granta, 2000.

Robert Hughes: *The Fatal Shore* published by Collins Harvill, 1987.

Phillip Knightley: *Australia: A Biography of a Nation* published by Jonathan Cape, 2000.

D.H. Lawrence: *Kangaroo* published by Cambridge University Press, 2002

John Douglas Pringle:

Australian Accent published by Chatto and Windus, 1958.

On Second Thoughts published by Angus and Robertson, 1971.

Have Pen Will Travel published by Chatto and Windus, 1973.
Eric Rolls:
Australia – A Biography published by University of Queensland Press, 2000.
Visions of Australia published by Lothian Books, 2002.
Susan Sickert:
Beyond the Lattice: Broome's Early Years, published by Fremantle Arts Centre Press, 2003.
Colin Thiele and Mike McKelvey:
Coorong published by Rigbys 1972
Range Without Man published by Rigby, 1974.
The Bight published by Rigby, 1976.

INDEX

285

INDEX

INDEX

Lightning Source UK Ltd.
Milton Keynes UK
UKHW012140251019
352309UK00010B/436/P